LEVERAGING LINKEDIN

For Job Search Success — 2019

FRED COON

WITH ANDREW R. KO & KELLY STEWART

GAFF Publishing

COPYRIGHT

Disclaimer and Legal Notices

CONTENTS

Don't Make These LinkedIn Mistakes

Getting Started with LinkedIn

Why Get LinkedIn?

Frequently, I hear that question. Not long ago, a friend asked me, "why should I bother with LinkedIn?" He wasn't a technologically challenged individual, so I was surprised that he should ask. My answer was simple, "It is the top social networking site for job seekers."

As Jeff Weiner, CEO of LinkedIn, explains it, "Post a full profile and get connected to the people you trust. Because if you're connected to those people and you posted a profile, then when other people are searching for people, they might find you."

With more than 600 million registered users–and adding two new members per second–the rate at which your network expands on LinkedIn can be truly amazing. A hundred strategic contacts could mean access to millions of people in a short amount of time. You'd have to attend dozens–or hundreds–of in-person networking events to equal the reach you can get on LinkedIn. Networking is hands down the best thing you can do for your career. Like Robert Kiyosaki says, "The richest people in the world look for and build networks; everyone else looks for work."

LinkedIn allows you to leverage the power of you network – the people you already know, and the people those people know – to help you connect to the person (or persons) who are in a position to offer you a job. As the cofounder of LinkedIn, Reid Hoffman, puts it, LinkedIn is about, "Connecting talent with opportunity on a massive scale."

Executives from all Fortune 500 companies are on LinkedIn. In addition, 59 percent of folks who are active on social networking sites say LinkedIn is their platform of choice, according to a June 2011 report from Performics and ROI Research. However, author Guy Kawasaki puts it best – "I could make the case that Facebook is for show, and LinkedIn is for dough."

Top 7 Reasons to Be on LinkedIn

1. FIND OTHER BUSINESS PROFESSIONALS.

Other social networks may try to focus on attracting professionals, but none compare with LinkedIn. Most are niche oriented. LinkedIn is not! Maybe that's because its membership has grown to over 600 million members since its launch in May 2003. No job seeker can afford to ignore its power, especially if the target job is with a younger company that is using social media in its marketing mix. People you know are already on the site, and so are people you should get to know, like recruiters and hiring managers.

2. DIG YOUR WELL BEFORE YOU'RE THIRSTY.

In his book of the same name, author Harvey Mackay advocates building your network before you need it. If you are presently employed, join LinkedIn now. That way you already have a network of connections in place when your job search begins. The best time to network is when you already have a job.

3. IT NEVER HURTS TO STRENGTHEN YOUR OFFLINE NETWORK.

We've all lost track of people over time. Often LinkedIn becomes a place you can reconnect. You find out what they are doing, where they work now, and whom they know–something that can be very important for a successful job search.

4. RECONNECTING WITH FORMER COWORKERS CAN LEAD TO WORK.

Staying in contact with former coworkers can be difficult. You might not be the only one who has had to move around! LinkedIn makes reconnecting easy in two ways. You can search by name and by employer. Now, that reference that you really wanted to locate might be as close as a reconnection.

5. ESTABLISH YOURSELF AS AN EXPERT.

Increasing your visibility is one of the ways you can position yourself as a thought leader in your industry. LinkedIn gives you a place to participate in Groups related to your expertise. Posting in Groups and participating in discussions can get you noticed and help build a positive reputation. When you actively engage in Groups on LinkedIn, other people may see your contributions to the discussions. These instances of you talking about what you know and demonstrating your knowledge is going to get you noticed. The people reading could easily be a hiring manager or a recruiter.

6. POSITION YOURSELF TO BE FOUND FOR JOBS WHEN YOU AREN'T EVEN LOOKING.

Being asked to interview for a job based on your LinkedIn profile happens often. As a passive candidate, your robust LinkedIn profile–filled with your accomplishments and strong keywords–often leads prospective employers to you. More and more recruiters are searching LinkedIn to find candidates that match their search assignments.

7. YOUR LINKEDIN PRESENCE HELPS WHEN SOMEONE "GOOGLES" YOU.

If you Google a friend of mine, Denise Rutledge, you'll discover that she has a lot of competition–from singer to a very nonbusiness like person. Because she chose her LinkedIn URL before any other Denise Rutledge optimized their account, she is the first Denise Rutledge to appear on Google's LinkedIn results. And that LinkedIn result is on the first page in web browser search results.

The point is that hiring managers and recruiters usually Google their job candidates. If you have an optimized LinkedIn profile, your chances of appearing on the first page on Google is high.

Ultimately, a LinkedIn profile is a resume, business card, and elevator speech condensed in one place. It's a powerful marketing tool – one you can't really afford to ignore.

Why LinkedIn Is Important for Your Job Search

CNN Money reported years ago that Accenture, a giant consulting firm, was going to forego the traditional methods of hiring headhunters or asking for employee referrals. The Company even decided to avoid the job boards. It went straight to LinkedIn.

Just suppose you had been a telecom consultant and didn't have a LinkedIn presence? You would not have been found for one of the 50,000 job openings Accenture had to fill.

This is a trend. You can see year after year LinkedIn's membership counts are only getting higher and higher. You can expect in the future that many businesses will do most of their own head hunting. And they are going to start on LinkedIn! Currently over 90 percent of companies and recruiters use LinkedIn for recruiting talent.

Once upon a time, attending networking mixers, industry events, and Chamber of Commerce meetings were the best way to make new connections and build business relationships. Now, these activities are online within the LinkedIn community. Much like networking in person, professionals interact on LinkedIn with the explicit intention of making business connections.

With LinkedIn, you get all the benefits of networking in person, with less of the hassle. Instead of going from business lunch to business lunch hoping to meet people, LinkedIn provides a platform for you to specifically search and re-search individuals whom you know will directly add value to your job search.

POWER TIP

Ensure your resume and LinkedIn profile are always in sync, as prospective employers are likely to Google you and compare the two.

We've already mentioned how employer and recruiters are using LinkedIn to locate both active job seekers and those who aren't necessarily looking (passive candidates). LinkedIn has more benefits. You have the ability to identify, research, contact, follow up, engage, and maintain your contacts in one place. In a world where information overload is a constant threat, that's a powerful organizational tool. No other platform has LinkedIn's ability to facilitate business networking. Facebook is for fun. LinkedIn is for business.

Since LinkedIn is a one-stop snapshot of you background, some suggest that your LinkedIn profile is more important than your resume. Howver, you should always recognize that your LinkedIn profile is not your resume. LinkedIn is a personal branding page. You need both a resume and a LinkedIn profile. When in a job search there are two types of employers: those who are using the latest technology, including social media, and those employers who prefer to post job openings in traditional ways. Savvy technology users often apply social media such as LinkedIn to narrow down the field of applicants that appear promising.

Keep your resume and LinkedIn profile in sync with one another, but they should not be exact copies of each other. Your resume and LinkedIn profile should agree on the positions you've held, your educational credentials, professional memberships, etc. but the content you include on your LinkedIn profile will be different from what you share on your resume. For one thing, a resume is limited in what it can share about you. Moreover, it should be tailored to a specific job. LinkedIn offers far more creativity in marketing yourself and your personal brand. We're going to share strategies you can use one LinkedIn to find a job. But first, we need to cover the basics of setting up a LinkedIn account.

How to Set Up a Basic Account

Setting up a LinkedIn account is a quick and easy process. However, speed is not the objective if you want to use LinkedIn to facilitate your job search. Rushing could lead to a sloppy profile that doesn't represent you well or may even prevent you from being called for an interview.

Basic memberships on LinkedIn are free. For most job seekers, the free option is adequate to effectively network on the site. If you find you need the paid upgraded account with the additional functionality, you can always upgrade your account later. To get started, go to LinkedIn.com. Fill in your first and last name, email address, and password. Then click **Join Now**.

Strategy Tip

Use your personal email address when you join LinkedIn not your work one. If you ever change your current employer, you will lose access to your LinkedIn account when your employer terminates your email account. You don't want to lose all of your hard work.

The email address you use should be for a web-based email account such as: Gmail, Yahoo, Outlook, etc.

Next, you'll be asked to apply a code via text or phone. Type the code in the space provided.

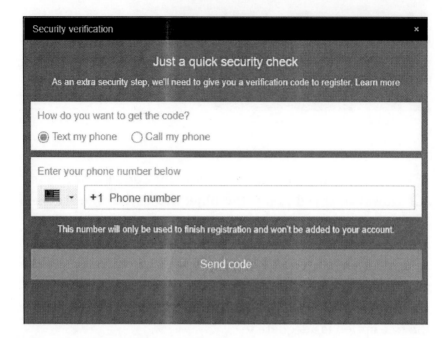

Once you've past this step LinkedIn will confirm your country and zip code. In the next step you'll be asked to select what your primary purpose is for using LinkedIn. Depending on which option you choose, it will determine what you see in the process of setting up your account. We'll choose "Finding a job" since that is the focus of this book.

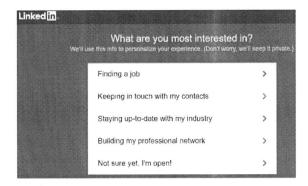

As another layer of security, you'll be asked to verify your email and input the 6-digit code that is sent to the email used to create the account.

Next you will be asked send connection requests to people you've communicated with in the past with the email you're using for this setup. You don't have to do this step now. If you skip it you can come back to this later. **By doing this step, LinkedIn will send connection requests to the people you've been emailing with and you will not have the opportunity to write a personalized message.** Be careful when doing this if you don't want connection requests going out to just anyone you've been emailing with.

LinkedIn encourages you to connect with as many people as you know and for a very good reason. The more people you're connected to and the larger your network, the more opportunities you'll find using LinkedIn. You're simply going to be more effective using LinkedIn if you can connect with more relevant contacts.

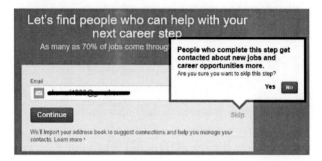

LinkedIn will then encourage you to create a job alert. You don't need to do this step now either. It can easily be done later once you begin searching for positions.

After skipping through these screens, LinkedIn prompts to upload your photo. Having a professional looking profile photo is very important for many reasons and we'll go in to them later but for now it is in your best interest to upload the most professional photo you have.

LinkedIn will now take you through a systematic process to build your profile. In reality, these first steps are about data mining LinkedIn is attempting to map you to others using your address book and other personal information.

We will control the building of your profile after we skip these steps. Again, you can add your contacts and control your connections later.

After you get passed these initial first steps of setting up a new account, you'll be at the point where you can choose to focus on development of your profile even further by continuing to input your professional background information, build your network, or follow sources of news and information.

Throughout the set-up process, LinkedIn will promote its paid Premium Account services asking you to try it for free for 30 days. The "Basic Account" (free) works for most people just starting out. Most functions that are available with a premium membership won't be important to you at this stage.

After you become familiar with LinkedIn, you can always upgrade later.

Take Action!

The next lesson will walk you through the process of building your LinkedIn profile. To prepare, you may want to gather the most important information about yourself. A resume is a handy reference tool when it comes to adding your employer, title and dates. You will also need a quality, professional photograph.

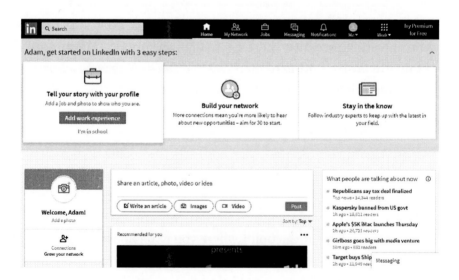

OPTIMIZING YOUR LINKEDIN PROFILE

O nce you start to develop your profile, LinkedIn is going to essentially walk you through the steps to get your profile set up and help you get noticed. LinkedIn encourages you to reach what they call "**All-Star**" status. You are 27 times more likely to be found in recruiter searches when you've reached this level. To get to this status you'll need to add 1) Your industry and location, 2) Your current or most recent position, 3) Two past positions, 4) Your Education, 5) A minimum of 3 skills, 6) A profile photo, and 7) At least 50 Connections.

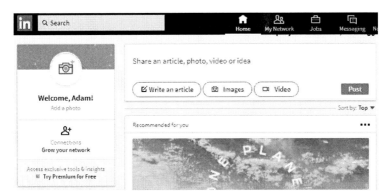

Here's how to find the page that shows your profile strength's status. Click on the area of your profile photo on your **Home** screen.

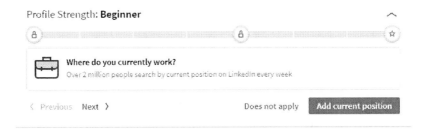

According to LinkedIn, the strength and completion level of your profile determines a member's All-Star status. Profiles that are 100 percent complete rank higher in search results versus those who have less complete profiles.

A well-written and complete LinkedIn profile is essential to maximizing LinkedIn's application to your job search efforts. The structure of a LinkedIn profile is like a traditional resume. LinkedIn treats the words you use to describe your experience and education as keywords. Applying the correct keywords will help your profile rank higher in search results. It works in much the same way as SEO (Search Engine Optimization). Profiles with more relevant keywords in them are going to appear higher in search results but SEO is not the only way to appear higher in search results on LinkedIn. Your activity and your connections also play a part of how high you show up in search results.

STRATEGY TIP

Have a current resume at your side to make sure you get dates and positions entered accurately.

Making Connections

In addition to your profile strength, your connections affect your LinkedIn search results. While it's important to make many connections, you don't want to spam people. (Don't connect with people for the sake of having significant connections. That's like giving your business card to *everyone* at a party.) You should strive to connect with people you know on LinkedIn, that's the easy part. It's in your best interest to identify and reach out to the people you DON'T know as well who would be strategic to your career goals and good people to know. Sometimes it's not who you know, it's who you know and who do THEY know. Find a way to get on their radar. If you simply send them a connection request make sure you write them a personalized note explaining why you're requesting to connect with them. They may accept or they might not. This is when having a good network is useful. LinkedIn is going to show you how you're connected to people when you use the search feature and search for **People**.

If you find someone who is a 2nd degree connection and you have connections in common, LinkedIn will show you who those people are. 2nd degree connections are the people who are in your extended network and you're connected by one degree of separation. You could reach out to any of these shared connections and ask them to introduce you to the person you're interested in contacting. This is why it is encouraged to connect with people you know. Someone can't likely introduce someone to another if they don't know them, that would be awkward. Reid Hoffman, co-founder of LinkedIn, is quoted as saying: "LinkedIn is a closed network, and for a very simple reason: For the network to have value as an introduction tool, the connections need to have meaning. It's up to you to vet each and every request so that if someone comes to you and says, 'Would you introduce me?' you're in a position to evaluate whether the connection would be of mutual benefit. "

Look at other LinkedIn profiles of people who have your job title. See what they're including in their profile that gets them a high ranking using LinkedIn's search algorithm.

Search – Using Google

How can you find profiles of individuals on LinkedIn who do what you do?

Use a Google search as a fast way to retrieve similar profiles.

1.   Go to Google.com.

2.   Type in the search string: "Site:Linkedin.com{yourjob title}".

3.   Replace "your job title" with your job title or keywords or terms related to your job or industry.

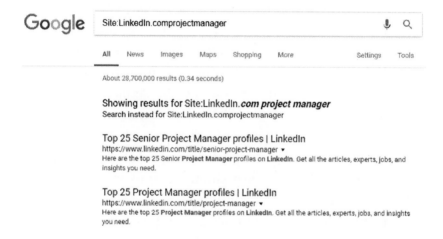

Ignore the ads and focus initially on the top 10 search results. Some of the links will lead to individuals and other to related categories or professionals. You can learn a lot by visiting the top-listed profiles. Pay particular attention to the headline the professional has used to describe him or herself. Take notes on the keywords they are using.

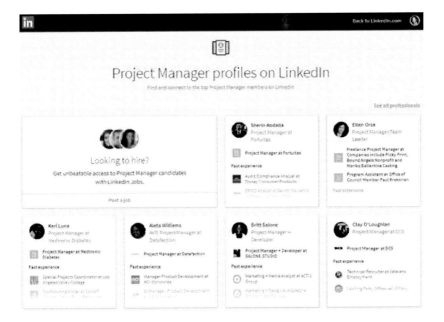

Also, you don't have to reinvent the wheel–if you have invested in a well-written professional resume, you will have most of the content you need to create a compelling LinkedIn profile.

Similar to other social media sites, LinkedIn uses its search algorithm to help connect you with people you might know or should know. For this reason, optimizing your profile so it ranks well in search results will help others find you.

Edit / Enhance Your Profile

Now that you have a better idea of what you want to include in your profile, it's time to start adding the information. There are several ways to create a profile.

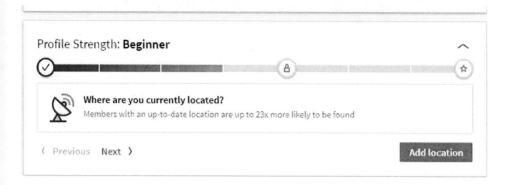

First, LinkedIn will give you the option to build your profile in any order you wish. The progress bar with prompt you to add different sections to add such as education and location.

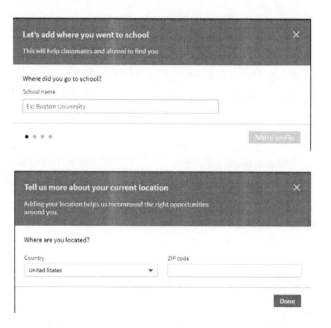

At this point you'll be prompted that you've reached the Intermediate level of profile strength. According to LinkedIn, with an Intermediate profile, you're 8 times more likely to get noticed by hiring managers and recruiters and 10 times more likely to be contacted.

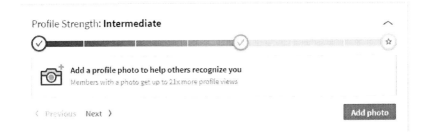

Your next move is to add a professional profile photo. Once you have a photo you want to use and upload it, you have some edit options such as *zoom* and *straighten* along with filters and other adjustments. I recommend not using filters. Keep in mind this

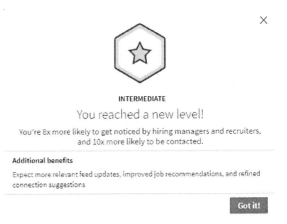

photo is supposed to represent you professionally. Filters may be fine for Facebook and Instagram, but LinkedIn is professional social networking and potential employers will be viewing this photo. It should and will be making first impressions.

Having a profile photo helps humanize you. If you have a professional photo, that's great but you don't need to spend a lot of money on a professionally taken headshot. Mobile phones these days have very good cameras in them. The camera in my phone is 12 megapixels, even better than my outdated DSLR. You can simply have a friend take a photo of you dressed professionally, in front of a neutral background, with good lighting and smile. We've all heard it since we were in grade school, "Smile for the camera" Studies have shown that a smile goes a long way in the performance of a profile photo. There is a helpful tool on the web at **Photofeeler.com** for some good information on real research on profile photos. You can read all about the research on the site and even upload your own photo to receive feedback on how "Competent", "Likable", and "Influential" your photo comes across.

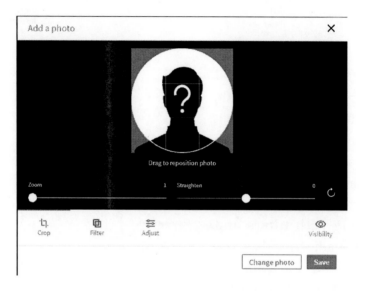

Your profile photo should reflect the image you want to present to others and for the industry you want to work in. Profiles with photos are 14 times more likely to be viewed verses incomplete profiles without photos.

Your next option is to add **Skills**. You're prompted to add 5 skills to start off. There are some who believe your **Skills** section is the most important part of your profile simply because of algorithms at work in the background of your profile that are linked to this section.

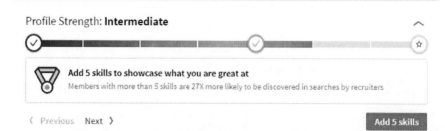

Depending on how many endorsements you have for the skills you have added, you'll see open positions relevant to those skills in your Jobs section. For example, if you have Sales listed as a skill and your connections have endorsed you many times for this skill, you'll start to see many sales positions in your view of the LinkedIn Jobs section.

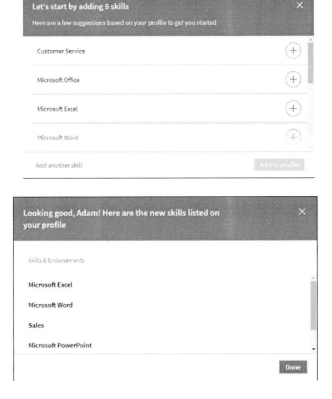

In the images above we can see a starter selection of skills which are transferable to many industries. You can select these or you can click on "Add another skill" to add whatever skill you choose and you could get more specific. Instead of just listing "Sales", you could list "Inside Sales" "Sales Training" or "Business Development" or you could list software relevant to your industry such as "Salesforce" or "PowerPoint." Whatever skills you choose to include, be mindful that these skills should represent what you do as a professional and what you're particularly skilled at.

You can list up to 50 skills and arrange them in any order you want. Consider your top 3 skills. What are they? These 3 skills are the first people will see when scrolling through your profile and come to this section. These 3 skills essentially would be part of your Personal Brand.

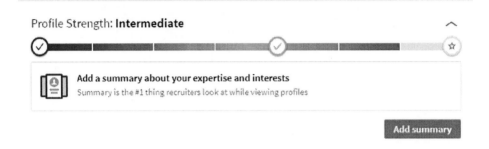

When you've finished listing your skills you'll be asked to add a **Summary**. You can always come back to this skills section later to add or remove skills as you wish. We'll discuss your **Summary** in more detail later. Once you've completed your summary you will have reached **All Star Status**.

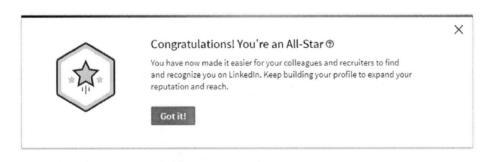

At any time during this process you can access different areas of LinkedIn and your profile. If you choose to do so you could scroll to different sections of your profile that you would like to edit. As shown in the following images, you will see a pencil icon next to the section. Click the pencil icon and LinkedIn will take you directly into edit mode. After making additions, edits, or deletions, be sure to click **Save**, otherwise your work will be lost.

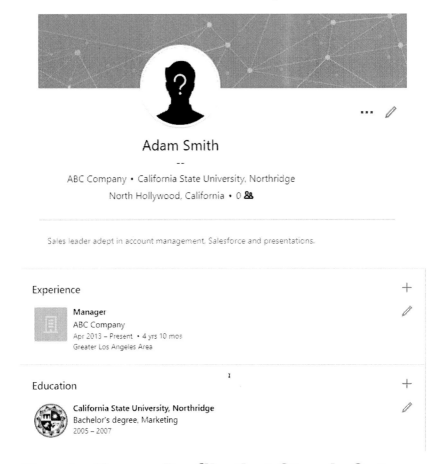

How to Have a Profile that Stands Out

Standing out with your LinkedIn profile can mean highlighting the strongest qualifications you have for an employer in your LinkedIn headline, backing up those qualifications with accomplishments throughout your profile summary, and using strategies that will help you be found by the people who most need someone like you.

Don't try to be all things to people. Although it is possible to create different versions of your resume to target different types of positions, you're limited to one LinkedIn profile. While it is technically possible to create a second LinkedIn profile using different credentials, that doesn't mean you should. There are at least a dozen articles about this and why it's not a good idea. On LinkedIn –as on your resume– one size does not fit all. Know your personal brand and use LinkedIn to market and promote you as the professional you are.

Perhaps the most challenging part of creating your LinkedIn profile is sounding original. By articulating what makes you unique and valuable, you will attract the attention of prospective employers. Be specific about what distinguishes you from others with a similar job title.

The answers to these questions may give you some ideas for creating your LinkedIn profile and headline:

- *What specific job titles are used to describe someone in your position? (Be specific regarding level, function role, and industry.)*

- *In performance reviews, in what areas do you receive the highest scores or the most positive feedback?*

- *What is the most important part of your current job?*

- *What is your biggest achievement in your job— have you saved your company money, helped the company make money, or helped it become more efficient, improve safety, improve customer service, etc.*

- *What are your top three skills?*

- *What are you best known for at work?*

- *If you were asked to select your replacement, what qualities would you be looking for?*

- *What kind of challenges at work do you most enjoy working on?*

- *Do you have any specific training or credentials that distinguish you?*

- *What makes you different from other (job titles)? Is there an area in which you are better than others?*

Can you distinguish yourself by the geographic area in which you work or through your years of experience?

Upload a Photo

If you skipped adding a photo earlier, you can upload your photo by clicking on where your profile photo would be from your profile view. Once you're in this section you have the option to zoom, straighten, crop, filter or adjust whichever photo you choose to upload by clicking

Change Photo. From here you would upload a photo just as you would any other site.

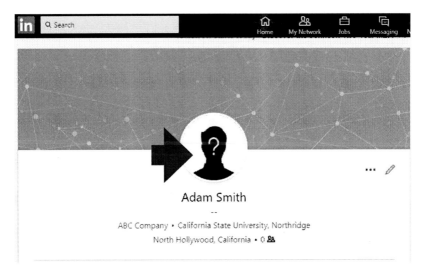

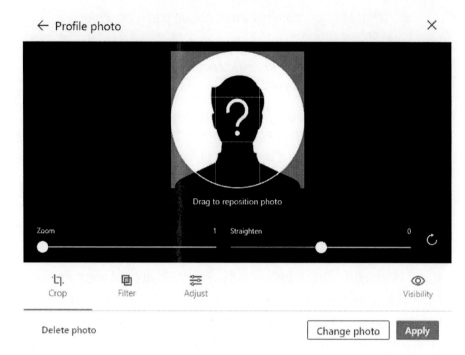

You can upload a JPG or PNG file. Square photos are ideal but you can always crop as needed. The maximum file size is 8MB and ideal photos are between 400 x 400 pixels and 20,000 pixels in height or width.

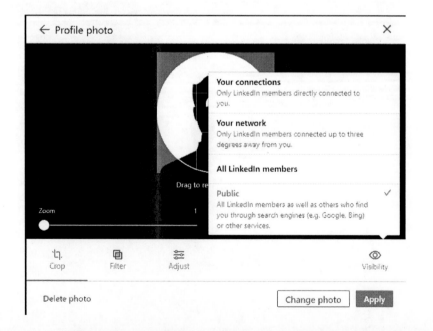

In the same place where you uploaded your photo, you have the option to designate if you want it to be viewable to only your connections, your network, all LinkedIn members, or public. Much like in other sections of the site, you can control the privacy of your content. This is my take on that, I'm not putting anything on LinkedIn that I'm not comfortable with the public seeing. I leave these settings alone. The object of LinkedIn when you're in job search is to be found and by the right people. You don't want to impede you chances of being found.

Hiring managers tend to make initial decisions in 5 to 7 seconds. So job seekers must establish "visual connectivity" in that amount of time. Strong profile pictures help to achieve this!

– **Jay Block**, President, The Jay Block Companies, LLC.

Jay's 6 Tips to Ensure the Right LinkedIn and Online Profile Picture

1. **Hire a professional.** A professional photographer can capture the essence of what job seekers want to portray. For a few hundred dollars, the return on investment can be invaluable.

2. **Choose a photo that looks like the job seeker.** When a job seeker appears at the interview, the interviewer should not be asking, "Where is your daughter?"

3. **The face ideally should take up about 60 percent of the frame.** Anyone can look good with the right photographer. A long distance picture of a job seeker on top of a mountain won't cut it.

4. **Choose the right expression.** Tyra Banks would say, "Smile with your eyes." Physiology is important when taking a picture. The picture should be energetic and engaging.

5. Job seekers should wear what they would wear to work (LinkedIn and websites). They should dress appropriately, even if the picture is simply a head and shoulder shot. They should wear clothes that match the level of attire for the positions they are seeking.

6. **Stand out professionally.** Again, a professional photographer can help here; black & white or color? What kind of background? Stand on your feet or on your head? What must one do to stand out professionally?

A picture tells 10,000 words. Make each word count.

Create Your Headline

Your LinkedIn headline is one of the most important parts of your profile. How you describe yourself to prospective employers and networking contacts is vitally important. When someone conducts a search on LinkedIn, a search result returns a listing displaying photos, names, and headlines. This is why it's important to have a good headline. A headline filled with the right keywords is an effective marketing and positioning tool. You may have heard that when you're in job search you have a job; it's in Sales and Marketing and you're the product. If you've selected your keywords effectively, it will help you show up higher in search results.

If you add a new employer that you designate as your current employer, LinkedIn updates your headline automatically to reflect the new employer unless you indicate you do not want it to.

Add experience ✕

Title

Company

Location

From
Month ▾   Present
Year ▾

☑ I currently work here
☐ Update my industry
☑ Update my headline

Share profile changes
Yes ⬤ If enabled, your network may see this change.

Save

Edit intro ✕

Adam   Smith
Add former name

Headline *
--

Current Position *
Manager at ABC Company ▾
Add new position

Education *
California State University, Northridge ▾
Add new education

Country *   ZIP code
United States ▾   91602

Locations within this area ▾

Your changes above won't be shared with your network

Save

LinkedIn will also update your status as you currently working at that company and update your industry as well. Again, you can turn these settings off if you want to. For example, Adam Smith is a Manager at ABC Company he recently got a new job at Fortune 500 Company and LinkedIn automatically reflects this in his headline (under his name), as well as his current employer above the city and state.

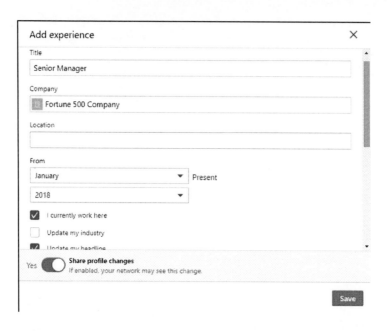

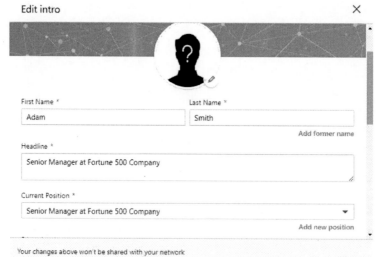

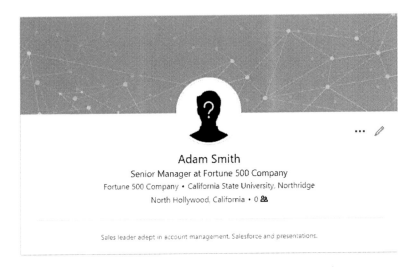

Adam Smith
Senior Manager at Fortune 500 Company
Fortune 500 Company • California State University, Northridge
North Hollywood, California • 0

Sales leader adept in account management, Salesforce and presentations.

Editing / Branding Your Headline

Today, branding statements are critical. What is your brand? Why are you unique?

Customizing your headline (under your name) to read as a personal branding statement is optional, but recommended. Simply go to your profile by clicking on your photo from the home screen. Next to your photo click on the pencil icon. You'll be given the option to customize your Headline.

Instead of the title of Senior Manager at Fortune 500 Company that the Headline defaulted to from what we just discussed, maybe we can use, *"Senior Sales Leader | Award winning sales professional | Certified Sales Trainer"* Type your unique Branding Statements in the box and click **Save**.

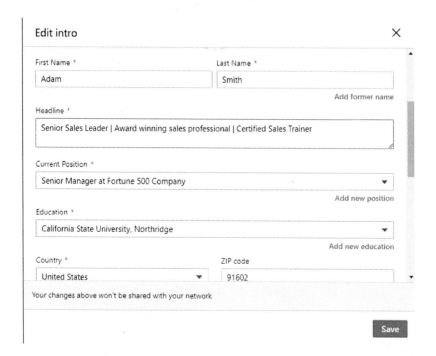

The character limit is 120 characters, so writing a focused headline is important. It's good to include keywords in your headline, but don't limit yourself to keywords because it will look a bit choppy.

Writing Attention-getting Headlines

The headline and the first two to three sentences of your LinkedIn profile Summary are critical to making connections and securing opportunities with recruiters and hiring managers.

Instead of focusing on yourself, focus on what you offer a prospective employer. The information you provide should be 80 percent about what you have done for your current employer (accomplishments-oriented) and 20 percent about you and what you're looking for. Unfortunately, most LinkedIn profiles (especially the summary section!) are the reverse.

Think of it this way: Prospective employers tune into a particular radio station – it's called "WIIFM." All employers are listening for "What's In It For Me?" (WIIFM). *Remember: Employers hire for their reasons, not yours.*

What proof do you have that you can offer the employer the results they are seeking? Quantify your accomplishments as much as possible in terms of numbers, percentages, and dollar amounts. Don't copy someone else's LinkedIn profile. Be original! Look at the other profiles for ideas, but don't copy someone else's headline or summary. Remember, your online presence must speak to your uniqueness. Also, give your profile some personality! People who make a connection with you through your profile are more likely to contact you about a career opportunity.

There are generally two schools of thought when it comes to writing your profile headline. The first is use a narrative or descriptive title; the second is to simply use keywords separated by commas, bullets or the pipe symbol (|) on your keyboard.

LinkedIn's current algorithm gives higher ranking to matching keywords, so strategy number two appeals more to computer searches, while strategy number one appeals to human readers. Eventually, a human being will review all profiles found through computer searches. It is important to balance readability with the inclusion of keywords.

You are limited to just 120 characters in your LinkedIn headline, so it's also important to be succinct and direct.

Things you can consider including in your LinkedIn headline:

➤ Job titles

➤ Types of customers/projects you work with

➤ Industry Specialization

➤ Brands you've worked for

➤ Certifications or designations

➤ Geographic territory specialization

Formulas for Writing an Effective LinkedIn Headline

One effective technique is to pull a quote from a reference you've received plus another important piece of information such as a specialty area.

Here are some strategies for writing your LinkedIn headline, along with the advantages and disadvantages that go along with each tactic.

1. SIMPLE

Say it simply and directly. Give your job title and the name of your employer. This is a good strategy if your job title is a strong keyword and /or the company you work for is well known. The advantage is that it clearly communicates who you are and what you do.

The disadvantage is that it doesn't set you apart from any others who could claim those same credentials.

Adam Smith
Senior Manager at Fortune 500 Company
Fortune 500 Company • California State University, Northridge
North Hollywood, California • 0 👥

This strategy can also use the following formulas:

➤ Job Title

➤ Job Title at Company Name

➤ Job Title for Industry at Company Name

➤ **Job Title** Specializing in **Keywords**

Here is an example of a headline that incorporates a job title and keywords:

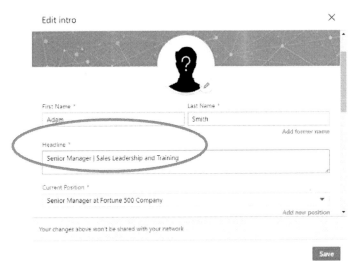

2. WHAT YOU DO

This strategy focuses on job functions instead of job titles. The advantage to this headline strategy is that job functions often make excellent keywords. The possible problem is you simply stringing together a bunch of job functions without creating a story to explain who you are -along with what you do–so make sure you add some context to your keywords/job functions.

This strategy can also incorporate key projects and/or the names of key clients or important employers, especially if any of those have high name-recognition value. You may also wish to include a specific industry or geographic area to your job function-focused head line.

Here is an example that uses job function and targets the kind of clients this professional serves.

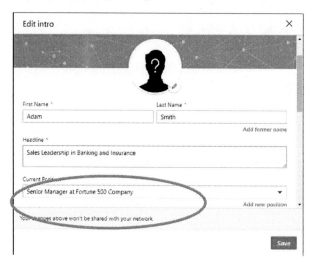

3. THE BIG BENEFIT

It's important to identify the primary benefit you have to offer a prospective employer. Target what author

Susan Britton Whitcomb says are "Employer Buying Motivators" in her book, *Resume Magic*. The 12 specific needs a company has include the company's desire to make money, save money, save time, make work easier, solve a specific problem, be more competitive, build relationships or an image, expand their business, attract new customers, and/or retain existing customers.

How can you be a problem solver for your next employer? Think about the job you want and what your next boss would want in an employee. <u>Make that the focus of your headline.</u>

This can be expressed in several different ways:

➤ (Job Title) That Gets (Results)

➤ (Adjective) (Job Title) With Recorded Success in (Results)

Be Specific! Adding numbers and other specific wording can make your LinkedIn headline much more powerful. Here is the same strategy, but this one quantifies the scope and scale of the benefit to the employer. Here are two examples:

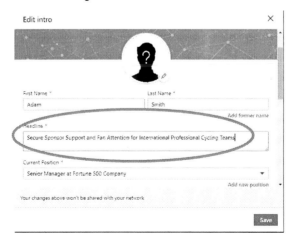

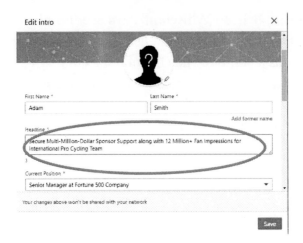

As you write your headlines, try not to include any of the Top 10 Overused Buzzwords in LinkedIn Profiles in the United States. Demonstrate that you truly are creative by finding a way to show it. If you want to highlight your creativity, find a way to show it. Saying you're creative, innovative, etc. wastes valuable real estate on your profile.

POWER USER TIP — BE UNIQUE

According to LinkedIn, these are the 10 most overused words/phrases on the site. Avoid using them in your headline and summary:

1. Problem Solver
2. Innovative
3. Motivated
4. Team Player
5. Dynamic
6. Proven Track Record
7. Results-oriented
8. Fast-Paced
9. Extensive Experience
10. Entrepreneurial

4 Top Headline Tips

When someone searches for you on LinkedIn, they see three things: Your name, your LinkedIn headline, and your location. Expect the decision to learn more about you to rest on the impression these three elements make on the hiring manager or recruiter.

1. **Compare your professional headline to a newspaper or magazine headline.** A headline should always hint at what will follow. The reader should have an idea of what your profile will include.

2. **Be specific.** It results in a much better headline. If you are vague, you won't grab the attention you desire.

3. **Great headlines attract attention.** The more people who view your profile, the better your chances of connecting with the right person who can lead you to your dream job.

4. **Identify your skills set.** Your headline needs to quickly identify you as a certain type of person – i.e., manager or executive, or someone who specializes in a certain field or industry.

A well-written headline will help you to structure the rest of the information you include in your LinkedIn profile. If the information doesn't support the headline, consider whether it should be included at all. Remember, focus is important.

NOTE: LinkedIn's default headline setting is your job title and the company you currently work. If you don't change it, this is what LinkedIn will show on your profile.

An Enthusiastic Testimonial

This headline strategy works best when you've received honors or recognition within your field. This can be an extremely effective strategy if you word it correctly. It's important that the designation is clear enough to stand on its own without too much detail. If it requires too much explanation, you may not have enough room within LinkedIn's 120-character limit.

A word of caution, however, don't use honors or recognition that are too far in the past. "Four-Time President's Award-Winner for Revenue Growth in the Ball Bearings Industry" isn't as impressive if those awards were for 1998, 2001, 2003, and 2005.

Andrew K.
"Andrew is impressive but more importantly, I felt inspired. He is very knowledgeable and has helped me in my success."
Lee Hecht Harrison • California State University-Northridge
Greater Los Angeles Area • 500+

This strategy also works if you can make a claim that is defensible (i.e., the statement is arguably true). Put the claim in quotes so it appears as if it has been published somewhere.

If you are having trouble writing your LinkedIn headline, write a very rough draft. It doesn't matter if it's not good or if you have to leave some blanks. Having a framework will make it easier for you to complete later.

Go ahead and finish writing the rest of your LinkedIn profile and then come back to it. Oftentimes, the headline will become much clearer at that point. Just remember to review your LinkedIn profile to make sure all the information you've included supports the focus of the content, as directed by the headline and summary.

You can also look on LinkedIn for inspiration. Check out the headlines and summaries of people you're connected with, or conduct a search for others in your field. Please do not simply copy their information; instead, use it as inspiration.

4. Years of Experience

Another strategy is to highlight the number of years you've been in your industry.

When appropriate, you might want to highlight a benefit you've consistently delivered. It's best to pick something that you know will show up in references.

Andrew K.

Career Leadership and Workforce Development | Executive Career Coach | Veteran's Career Coach | Trainer and Facilitator

Lee Hecht Harrison • California State University-Northridge

Greater Los Angeles Area • 500+

When you are through with your headline, it should accomplish four things:

> ❯ It should be as powerful as a newspaper headline

> ❯ It should be specific

> ❯ It should attract the type of interest you want to draw

> ❯ It should be clear what your skill set is

LinkedIn Success Stories

John actively maintained his LinkedIn profile. He received two to three invitations a week to consider openings. One of those openings was a position at IBM. He interviewed and was offered the job.

David went to networking events and followed up on LinkedIn with all the contacts he made. When he was laid off, he updated his LinkedIn status with "I'm up for grabs. Who wants me?" He received a phone call that same morning with a job offer. Within a week, he was back to work. Later when he was ready for a new opportunity, he was able to once again tap into his LinkedIn network. Within two weeks, he had found the opportunity that fit him.

When Kristen Jacoway moved to South Carolina, she didn't know anyone. She found a company she was interested in working for. The head of HR was a 2nd degree connection. She clicked on her name and discovered which one of her 1st degree connections could introduce her. Within a week she had an interview. A week later she was hired to provide contract work for the company.

Choose Skills

You may include up to 50 skills in your profile. Choose the skills that your connections can verify. In addition, stick with skills that enhance your value. For example, Adam Smith may be a great cook, but those skills have nothing to do with his sales career.

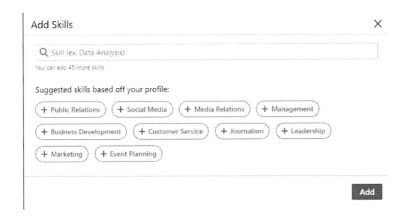

As you start typing in a skill, LinkedIn will recommend related skills. You'll want to consider using these because they are already in LinkedIn's keyword bank. That means people are using them to find others.

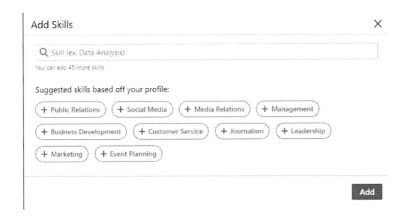

Just because you can add 50 skills doesn't mean you have to. Keep focused on your goals. You don't want to come across as a "Jack of all trades and master of none" type. Emphasize the skills you do best.

Once you list your skills, your connections can endorse them. Your connections can also endorse you for skill you haven't thought of on your own.

You have the choice of showing your endorsements or keeping them hidden. LinkedIn will display up to 99 connections who have endorsed you for a skill.

Today we live in a click happy society and it is very easy to endorse a connection for skills when we view a profile. Because of this, endorsements are not as valuable as recommendations.

Describe Your Current and Past Positions

LinkedIn's advice to choose two or three things to emphasize about each position is a solid strategy. Most people try to stuff too much information into this section. Emphasize those things that made the greatest difference in that position. For example, as a resume writer, what would you want to know about me before you hired me? Likewise, with your previous position, emphasize as much as possible those aspects of the job that enhance the perception that you have the skills to write the kind of resume that gets results.

You are laying a foundation for the types of references you will look for at a later stage. You can seek out prior clients or colleagues that you've helped or who will validate your expertise and value. Rather than trying to build yourself up, think about what others will say about you, and use that as a starting point.

You can always come back and revise based upon the references you actually receive.

You'll be given a new list to check off after you share your profile (or opt out). LinkedIn will:

➤ Check to see if you have any additional education to add to your profile

➤ Ask you if you know any other languages

➤ Ask you to add a summary of who you are and your objectives

Experience

Senior Manager
Fortune 500 Company
Jan 2018 – Present • 1 mo
Greater Los Angeles Area

Manage business development on high-net-worth accounts for a a Fortune 500 company.
- Develop relationships with clients, industry leaders and vendors.
- Analyze industry trends, use best practices and informed decisions that meet the needs of clients and the company.
- Manage a sales team to ensure department goals are met.

Writing Your Summary

After the headline, the most-often read section of your profile is the summary. LinkedIn allows up to 2,000 characters in your summary. Use them wisely-and use all of them! When you get started on writing your summary you'll want to expand the size of the text box. Look for the little arrow at the lower right-hand corner. Take you mouse and drag it to enlarge the section. Doing this will make it easier to write and edit your content.

Your summary is the first section your readers have to read all about what you do, what sets you apart from other professionals in your industry and why they should continue reading or even reach out to contact you. It's not enough to be found by recruiters and hiring managers. You want to be found AND impress those who find you. Think of your **summary** as an elevator pitch. You have 2,000 characters and spaces to talk about your professional background or skill in much more detail and personality than you would on your resume. You want your summary to grab the attention of the reader. Be mindful of the keywords you're using in this section. You listed your skills in the section before this, now you'll want to expand on what you do best. Using the keywords that are relevant to your industry and profession will help you in searches when someone is looking for a candidate like you. Search Engine Optimization is very much at play here and in other sections of your profile. The more you include relevant keywords in your profile that someone might use to find someone like you when they perform a candidate search, the more likely you are to show up higher in those search results. Including relevant keywords isn't the only way to help you show up higher in search results buts it's one of the easiest things you can do to optimize your profile to help you be found.

Viewers only see the first two lines of a user's summary when they view someone's profile. They have to click on "show more" to read the whole summary. You'll want to have an impactful first sentence to hook the reader and get them wanting to read more about you. Remember when you're in job search you have a job, it's in sales and marketing and you're the product.

Another strategy to consider when developing this **summary** section of your profile is grabbing the attention of the reader from the start and including rich media. You might consider uploading photos, videos, presentations, documents, or other forms of rich media to make your profile stand out. This content should be relevant to what you do as a professional and aim to impress and it should supplement the text sections of your LinkedIn profile. An example might be if you're a sales leader to not only talk about your drive to meet and exceed sales goals but perhaps you can include awards you've received or client testimonials. **According to LinkedIn, your summary is the #1 section of your profile recruiters look at.**

Summary

> In the competitive world of professional cycling the competition isn't limited to the athletes in the peloton. The teams themselves are also competing - for sponsors, fan attention, media coverage, race invitations, and social media status.
>
> In my role as Team CycleProSports' National PR Rep. I grew the team's social media presence by more

One format that is very effective is the Who/What/Goals structure. You begin with **Who** you are, **What** you have to offer (what is unique about you or your experience?), and what **Goals** you have for your career of for being on LinkedIn.You may repeat this pattern numerous times throughout the summary by dedicating one sentence to Who, one to Why, and one to Goals.

Another effective formula is to shift to a how focus after you have written your Who/What Goals opening. This is especially effective for consultants and service providers. You might find it difficult to use all 2,000 characters at first. Don't worry about it. It is better to write a tight summary than to ramble on to meet a character quota. In the example shown in the next screenshot, there are just over 1,000 characters. Remember, you can always revisit your summary and expand it.

Edit intro   ✕

Summary

*CORPORATE COMMUNICATIONS & MEDIA RELATIONS: Trusted advisor, credentialed coach, and savvy strategist of corporate communications and media relations. Audience seer and dragon slayer of employee trances caused by boring, corporate-lingo. Fan of messaging that use purposeful talking points, presentations, content marketing and brand journalism pieces that zero in on what people care about. Develop press releases, media inquiries, articles, position papers, opinion pieces, etc. Write to express, not impress!

*COMMUNITY OUTREACH & EMPLOYEE ENGAGEMENT: Leader of measured engagement and recognition experiences that revitalize soul in the workplace and mirror a company's values to gain trust. Natural behaviorist and neutral diplomat in pinpointing breakdowns and rebuilding bridges that form a culture everyone wants: inspiring, happy, transparent, high-performing, and yes, profitable.

*HR, TALENT DEVELOPMENT, & RECRUITMENT: Restoring "human" back into "resources" for companies that realize you can still mitigate risk while nurturing a culture of humanity and autonomy. Sharp trouble-shooter with a sixth sense in identifying where a company is having trouble with the curve. Credentialed coach with rich experience in talent planning and development, change management, post-merger integration, recruitment, and behavior/career assessment and interpretation. Let people master what they do best!

Your changes above won't be shared with your network

Save

Additional Summary Writing Tips

The first two or three sentences need to instantly get your prospects interested in your profile or, even better, get them excited about reading the rest of your profile. Your LinkedIn summary can set you apart from other job seekers on LinkedIn by demonstrating that you understand what employers want and what you have to offer that meets that need.

To do this you must address specific questions every prospect is asking:

➤ How will you add more value to this company, or solve problems better than other job candidates?

➤ How will your next employer benefit by hiring you? Quantify the value in terms of numbers, money, and/

or percentages. Use specific numbers and facts to build credibility.

➤ What experience can you offer that will provide value to your next employer?

➤ What additional skills do you have that set you apart from other candidates with a similar background?

Write naturally and conversationally. In contrast to your resume, it is okay to use pronouns such as "I, me, or my" in your summary if you wish. Of course, you would not in your resume. Regardless, whether you use or exclude pronouns, speak in the first person, not third person. For example, "I did such and such. Write as if you're speaking to an individual reader. Make it personal. Be sure to emphasize outcomes as well as what makes you uniquely qualified to do the job you do. Try to find a common thread that connects all of your work experiences. Then, once you have a theme, use storytelling principles to write your summary a narrative. Have a beginning, a middle, and an end.

Your summary can be anywhere from a few sentences up to a few paragraphs. Nevertheless, don't waste any words. Make the most dramatic, powerful, attention-getting statement possible. Don't use more words than necessary, and avoid flowery language. The point of the first sentence is to get the prospect to read the second sentence... the next one... and the next.

Edit intro   ✕

In the competitive world of professional cycling the competition isn't limited to the athletes in the peloton. The teams themselves are also competing - for sponsors, fan attention, media coverage, race invitations, and social media status.

In my role as Team CycleProSports' National PR Rep. I grew the team's social media presence by more than 25% in one year. This included facilitating more than 12 million fan engagement opportunities online. I also secured stories in all major cycling industry trade outlets and consumer-facing publications including ProCycling Monthly" "Biking News" "Two-Wheeler" and "ProVelo"

I also handled crisis communication for the team including the controversial finish of the Tour of Africa and media relations after the bankruptcy of one of the team's major sponsors. The team's owner recognized this effort with a handwritten letter praising my "responsiveness, tact, and diplomacy in effectively handling what could have been a disaster" for the team.

I am currently pursuing offers for the 2012 -13 season. (As an independent contractor, I work exclusively with one team each year on a contract basis.) If your professional cycling team is looking to increase your team's profile in the media with fans and online, I would love to talk with you about what I can do for you. Click on the website link in my profile for full contact information.

I am also interested in connecting with you on Linkedin if you are a journalist or blogger who covers professional cycling, a race organization official or sponsor, or UCI or USA Cycling-accredited official.

Your changes above won't be shared with your network

Save

Be conversational and informal in your tone. Use contractions ("you're instead of "you are"). Every word counts! Pay attention to grammar and spelling. Make sure there are no mistakes in your profile. Re-read and edit it. Have a colleague, friend, or spouse read it. Copy and paste it into a word processing program and run a spell-check on it.

You can also use asterisks, dashes, hyphens, and other keyboard characters to format the summary and make it easier to read. Notice these elements in the summary above written by Fred Jobseeker.

Notice the format:

> ➤ In the opening paragraph, draw attention to issues, challenges, or problems faced by your prospective employer.

> ➤ In the second and third paragraphs, demonstrate the value you offer to employers by quantifying the accomplishments in your current position (ideally related to the problems outlined in the first paragraph).

> ➤ In the fourth paragraph, talk about why you might be open to inquiries (if you are a passive candidate). If you are unemployed, you might state the reason your most recent position ended (if the company closed, for example) or that you are available immediately.

> ➤ Give the reader information on how to contact you. Instead, direct them to connect with you on LinkedIn or use one of your links to provide a method for direct contact.) You can also use the Contact and Personal Information section to provide a phone number and/or email address.

Using these strategies, you can develop a LinkedIn headline and summary that will lead to job opportunities, contacts from prospective employers and recruiters, and increased visibility online for your job search.

Upload Work Samples or Projects

There are two ways to highlight different projects. You can upload a file or insert a link (video, images, other documents, PowerPoint, SlideShare, etc. as part of the summary section or under each job of the Experience section. This is a way to highlight visually and/or audibly some of the things you have done.

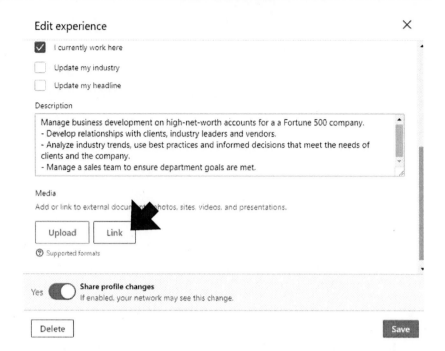

The second way is to fill out the Projects section. This is a subsection of the **Accomplishments** section of your profile we'll discuss later. If you choose to link to a project, LinkedIn will ask you to create a title for your project.

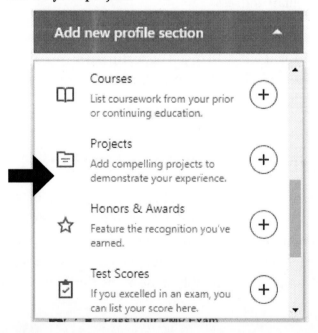

Choose a title that uses keywords for your industry, if possible. At the same time, don't sacrifice clarity on what the work sample will demonstrat. Keep the title on target for the content.

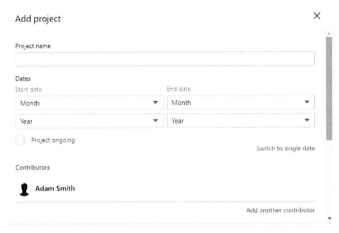

LinkedIn also allows you to add your connections who were involved in the project with you and highlight your whole team.

The Projects section is the perfect place to share examples of your work. If you don't have any projects, you may skip this section, yet it really is worth creating a special work sample or project just for LinkedIn for some careers or industries.

For example, a writer wouldn't want to miss this opportunity to share examples of articles that have landed notoriety for a client (of course, unless it was published, she or he would change identifiable information).

Accomplishments

This section allows you to include many aspects of your professional self that help you stand out from others. It allows you to showcase your hard work to strengthen or reinforce your personal brand. It forms an easily viewable list of accomplishments to sell and market the product of you.

> Projects you've worked on

> Course work you've taken

> Honors or Awards you've won

> Certifications you've achieved

> Organizations you belong to

> Publications, Test Scores and Patents

It used to be that each of these items in this Accomplishments section was its own section you could add to your profile but now having them all in one place one can simply scroll through and click on what they would like more information on.

Add Courses

Now, you have the opportunity to highlight courses that demonstrate you have domain knowledge of your field. These courses don't have to be from one of the formal educational institutions you've attended.

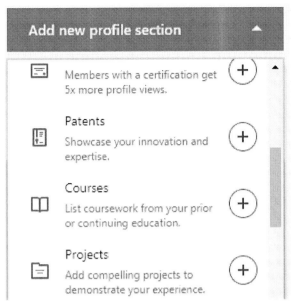

To add a course, click on "Add new profile section" on the right-hand side while viewing your profile. Scroll down to select **Accomplishments** and select what you would like to add. In this case we're adding "Courses".

While this is optional, it's a good place to include training you've taken that isn't necessarily issued by an educational institution. Perhaps you completed employer-based training. You may add independent coursework or classes taken through an external association.

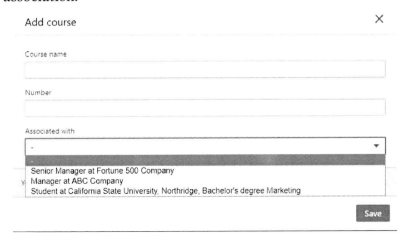

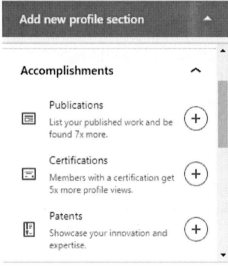

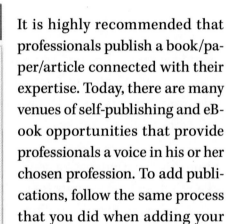

It is highly recommended that professionals publish a book/paper/article connected with their expertise. Today, there are many venues of self-publishing and eBook opportunities that provide professionals a voice in his or her chosen profession. To add publications, follow the same process that you did when adding your courses.

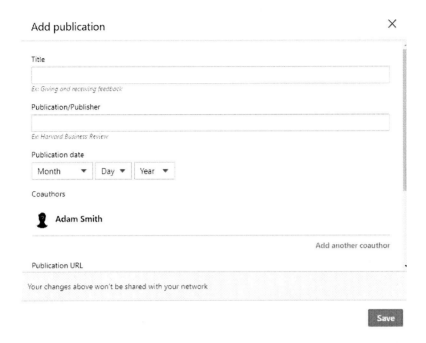

If you have not published an eBook through one of the main publishers such as Kindle or CreateSpace, you can provide the URL to the page from which potential clients or customers can download the eBook.

At this point, you have completed the meat of your profile. If you see other categories that you would like to add notable accomplishments, by all means, do so. As you continue to use LinkedIn, it will ask you to add more positions.

If you don't have additional positions to add, there is one strategy you might be able to use. For example, if you have worked for the same business for 10 years, yet changed positions within the business during that time, consider breaking up your experience to reflect this. It demonstrates progression in your career–always a good thing!

Another area that LinkedIn will consider incomplete is your connections. You will have to continue looking for connections until you have met the minimum quota of 50.

Complete your LinkedIn Profile. It is important!

Use this Checklist to make sure you haven't missed anything:

- ✓ Basic profile activities
- ✓ Profile photo
- ✓ Your current industry
- ✓ A current position with description
- ✓ Two or more positions
- ✓ Education
- ✓ At least five skills
- ✓ 50+ connections
- ✓ A summary

Most Important

➤ **Proofread** your profile carefully. Check grammar and spelling!

➤ **Update your profile regularly.** Not only will your connections be notified when you update information on you profile (bringing you profile additional visibility), but you'll also be confident that someone searching for you will have access to the most current information.

Job Search Specific Activities

➤ Customize your LinkedIn profile URL (**www.linkedin. com/in/yourname**). By doing so you can use this customized URL in your email signature, resume, and business card. You want to make it easy for people to find you on LinkedIn. Directions to do this are found in the next section of this book.

➤ If you're including a link to your website or blog in the Contact and Personal Info section, customize the text link (rename it so it doesn't just say "personal website" or Company Website"). To do this select "other" from the dropdown and a space will appear below to type in what you would like it to be called.

➤ Include your contact information. LinkedIn allows you to add your phone number (designated as home, work, or mobile), your Twitter address, Instant Messenger contact information (AIM, Skype, Yahoo Messenger, ICQ, Google Hangouts, QQ or WeChat), and your email address.

Take Action!

Focus on completing your profile so you can achieve All-Star profile strength. Not everyone logs into LinkedIn every day, and sometimes you may feel impatient waiting for people to accept invitations. It will take some time to meet LinkedIn's connection quota.

Keyword Basics

Keywords play an important part in helping people you may not know, find you- this is particularly true for job seekers who are hoping for contacts from prospective employers and recruiters.

LinkedIn headlines are searchable fields using the People Search function when someone is looking for particular skills, interests, qualifications or credentials. They help others find you!

What are keywords

Keywords are words and phrases related to your work. They help a prospective employer find you when they need someone with those skills.

Where can you find keywords?

Brainstorm them. Write down a list of words that relate to you, your work, industry, and accomplishments. Try to come up with as big of a list as you can; you will narrow it down later.

You can also find keywords in job postings or job descriptions. Check out online job boards for positions. Don't worry about where the job is located; just find positions that are similar to the one you're seeking and write down the keywords.

You can also find broad job descriptions - with plenty of key-words – in the U.S. Department of Labor's free Occupational Outlook Handbook (**http://www.bls.gov/ooh/**).

Another great research tool is Google's AdWords Keywords Tool, which is found at: **http://adwords.google.com/select/keyword-ToolExternal**. You can use keywords you identified through your earlier research. Google AdWords suggests related keywords and tells you how popular those keywords are in current Googles search results.

How do you choose keywords?

You need to pick the Top 10 keywords that you will use in your LinkedIn headline and profile. The keywords that you select for you profile must fit two criteria: They must speak to your "onlyness" – what you want to be known for. This is part of your Personal Brand. And they must align with what employers value – what they want. Focusing on these areas enables you to get the most out of your online efforts while differentiating you from other job candidates with the same job title. You need to express clearly: "I am this." Someone who is reading your LinkedIn profile should be able to recognize you in it. If what you wrote could apply to anyone with your job description, revise what you've written.

PRIVACY

You have the option of restricting certain parts of your LinkedIn profile so the public cannot view them. In the past, LinkedIn users had more control over which LinkedIn members could view their profile. Now, the restrictions are more limited, and when you change your privacy settings, LinkedIn is referring to your privacy across Google or other major search engines.

When you are in active job search, you want your privacy settings to be as open as possible to encourage more profile views and connections. Google indexes LinkedIn profiles, so having an open profile can gain additional visibility through Google. A public profile on LinkedIn presents your professional skills to those who want to know more about you.

However, if you are currently employed, you want to consider your privacy settings more closely. You might want to limit viewing of your profile to direct connections or connections within your network.

Customizing Your LinkedIn URL

Change your public profile display by clicking on the "Edit public profile & URL" bar which is located on the right-hand column of your profile while viewing your profile.

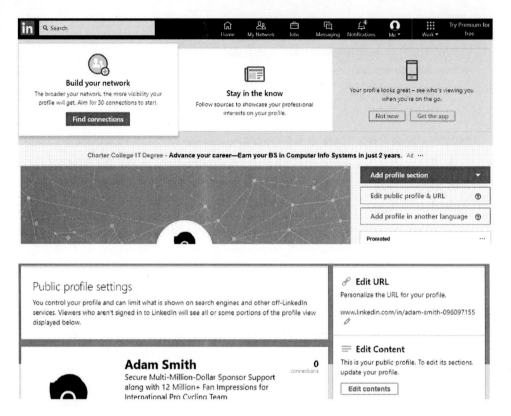

In your Public profile settings view, you'll find your default URL on the top right-hand side column. It's recommended that you customize your URL to something easily identifiable to you or something that resonates to your career goals because you want to make finding you as easy as possible. While this appears to have little to do with privacy, changing your LinkedIn URL makes you more visible. You always want to create a unique URL. To do this click on the pencil icon directly after the default URL that is there. Your cursor will appear directly after the **www. linkedin.com/in/** all LinkedIn URLs begin with this. You have anywhere from 5 -30 letters or numbers to work with. Spaces, symbols, or special characters are not allowed. That means no hyphens or underscores.

If your name is used by someone else, LinkedIn will let you know it is invalid.

Rather than using a URL with a number behind it, use a keyword related to your expertise. This is especially helpful to service providers who want to grow their exposure on LinkedIn within a certain niche, yet is also useful for anyone who works in a profession such as accounting, sales or one of the medical professions. For example, as a salesperson, Adam Smith could use "AdamSmithsSells" as a good URL. Both Google and LinkedIn will recognize the separate words. Once you've customized this URL it's something that you can use to market or promote you. You can put it on a business card, your email signature, and your resume. This is changeable in the future in case you need to alter the name you are using (for instance, in case of marriage, etc.)

Additional information that matters to you is on the right. Under the "Edit URL" section we just discussed. You'll see a section that reads: "Edit Content". As the title might suggest, this will take you back to your Profile view of your profile so you can edit the different sections of your profile. Under this is a section that reads: "Edit Visibility". This is where you can control who sees your profile. Its default is Public view but you can also select: "All LinkedIn Members", "Your network", or "Your connections". Public view will allow your LinkedIn profile to show in Google searches. You may or may not care about this depending on what your goals for being on LinkedIn are. When switching between these visibility modes LinkedIn will update your settings but search engines can take some time for these changes to register and refresh. LinkedIn does not control the refresh process.

Changing Your Privacy Settings

Notice the options you can deselect from public view. To obtain maximum exposure as an unemployed job seeker, make your profile visible to everyone. When your job search is complete, you can adjust your privacy settings and decide if there is information that you want to more closely control.

The default settings are best for active job seekers or individuals who use their LinkedIn profiles to promote their services. Under this is a list of different sections that you the user can choose to show or not show on your Public profile when choosing what to have visible on your public profile keep in mind the changes are not immediate. You can also choose to create a public profile badge if you wish to.

Advanced Privacy Settings

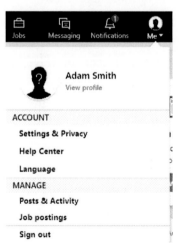

The privacy settings page is where you drill down to specific privacy details. This page allows you to customize all elements of your personal data. Image 6.5

To get to this page, move your mouse to your photo with "Me" under it in the top black ribbon of LinkedIn. Click to open the drop-down then click Settings & Privacy.

This will take to you to the page that gives you a different way to control your Profile, your Email Preferences, and other details. By default, the Account tab is selected when you visit the page for the first time.

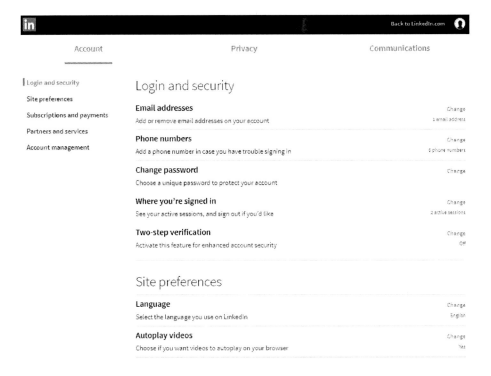

Under the "Privacy" tab You will see a list of a lot of different areas you can control.

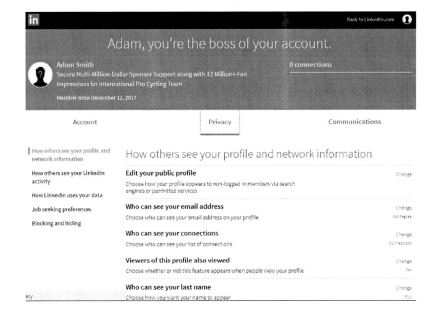

At the top of the list of options is **Edit your public profile** this will take you back to the section we just discussed. Under this is **Who can see your email address**. This defaults to your 1st degree connections but you can change this to: Only you, 1st and 2nd degree connections, or Everyone on LinkedIn.

Next down this section is **Who can see your connections.** LinkedIn gives you two options when it comes to whether people can see your connections: **Your connections** or **Only you**. You may not want to allow people to see who you're connected to. It's your choice. You can choose to allow your 1st degree connections to view your connections or make it so only you can see your connections. I equate this to playing nicely in the sandbox. Most of the people on LinkedIn are on it to network. LinkedIn is modern day networking. If you connect with someone, you most likely will get to see who they are connected to. It's how LinkedIn is supposed to work. If you have this privacy setting to "Only you" they will not have the benefit of viewing who you're connected to.

Who can see your connections

Choose who can see your list of connections

Members will still be able to see connections who endorse you and connections they share with you. (Don't want your endorsements visible? Just choose to opt out) Learn more

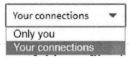

You may choose if you want to see the **Viewers of this profile also viewed** box on your profile page. This feature shows you profiles of others who were also viewed by people who viewed the profile you happen to be viewing at that moment while in the People Search view.

Viewers of this profile also viewed

Choose whether or not this feature appears when people view your profile

Should we display "Viewers of this profile also viewed" box on your Profile page?

Yes

The **Who can see your last name** option controls what you might guess by the title. It defaults to first and last but you can switch it to first and just last initial.

The next two options relate to visibility both on and off of LinkedIn. **Representing your organization** and **Profile visibility off LinkedIn.** For maximum visibility make sure they are switched to "Yes".

With the **Microsoft Word** option on you are opting in for your LinkedIn profile to help make Microsoft Word's new resume assistant more accurate.

Account	Privacy
How others see your profile and network information	**Representing your organization** Choose if we can show your profile information on your employer's pages
How others see your LinkedIn activity	**Profile visibility off LinkedIn** Choose how your profile appears via partners' and other permitted services
How LinkedIn uses your data	**Microsoft Word** Choose whether work experience descriptions from your LinkedIn profile can be shown in Resume Assistant, a feature within Microsoft Word.
Job seeking preferences	
Blocking and hiding	

How others see your LinkedIn activity

Profile viewing options
Choose whether you're visible or viewing in private mode

Manage active status
Choose who can see when you are on LinkedIn

Sharing profile edits
Choose whether your network is notified about profile changes

Profile viewing options is where you control how you are visible to others when you have viewed their profile. The question comes up often in workshops about why people choose to be "anonymous". While it may be slightly disturbing to some to see people viewing their profile when they don't know who they are but there are legit business reasons for doing so. They could be a recruiter or someone from a company the candidate applied to and they may not want the candidate knowing they are checking out their LinkedIn profile. We've no doubt learned by now employers are almost certainly using LinkedIn to check out potential employees. Just know if you choose to view other in **Private mode** / **Anonymous**, you won't be able to see who has viewed you either, unless you have a Premium membership.

Profile viewing options   Close
Choose whether you're visible or viewing in private mode   Full profile

Select what others see when you've viewed their profile

Your name and headline

○ Adam Smith
   Secure Multi-Million-Dollar Sponsor Support along with 12 Million+ Fan Impressions for International Pro Cycling Team
   North Hollywood, California | Entertainment

Private profile characteristics

○ Someone at California State University, Northridge

Private mode

○ Anonymous LinkedIn Member

Selecting Private profile characteristics or Private mode will disable Who's Viewed Your Profile and erase your viewer history.

Upgrade to Premium to see all your viewers in the last 90 days while browsing in private mode.

Under this is **Manage active status.** Switching this option on to "yes" will allow others to see if you're active on LinkedIn or available on the mobile LinkedIn app. The default is "no".

Manage active status
Choose who can see when you are on LinkedIn

○ Your Connections only
Only your 1st-degree connections will be able to see when you are on LinkedIn.

○ All LinkedIn members
All LinkedIn members will be able to see when you are on LinkedIn.

○ No one
No one on LinkedIn will be able to see when you are on LinkedIn.

Changes to this setting may take up to 30 minutes to take effect.

The next option you can control moving down the list is **Sharing profile edits**. It is recommended that you turn this off when you're developing your profile and / or editing sections of your profile because every time you save in a section it will generate an update. That said, Your network may *not* be notified right away of any changes you make. This is because we optimize notifications that are sent to your network based on their setting preferences. **Note:** It may take up to 12 hours for job change updates to be shared with your network.

By switching this to "No" you will no longer share profile changes with your network. They also will not see when you follow companies or make recommendations.

Actions on your profile that are shared with your network	Actions on your profile that are NOT shared with your network	
■ Add a new or current position	■ Headline	■ Skills
■ Edit an existing or current position	■ Intro	■ Publications
	■ Contact info	■ Certifications
■ Celebrate a work anniversary	■ Past positions	■ Courses
	■ Education	■ Projects
	■ Volunteer experience	■ Test scores
		■ Organizations
	■ Languages	■ Patents

Once your profile is fully developed, you should revisit this option and switch it back to "Yes" so your activity can be viewed by your network. If you're in job search, this is wise.

Job Seeking Preferences

Privacy

How LinkedIn uses your data

Download your data
Download an archive of your account data, posts, connections, and more

Manage who can discover your profile from your email address
Choose who can discover your profile if they have your email address

Manage who can discover your profile from your phone number
Choose who can discover your profile if they have your phone number

Sync contacts
Manage or sync contacts to connect with people you know directly from your address book

Sync calendar
Manage or sync calendar to get timely updates about who you'll be meeting with

Salary data on LinkedIn
See and delete your salary data

Social, economic and workplace research
Choose whether we can make some of your data available to trusted services for policy and academic research

Privacy

Job seeking preferences

Let recruiters know you're open to opportunities
Share that you're open and appear in recruiter searches matching your career interests

Sharing your profile when you click apply
Choose if you want to share your full profile with the job poster when you're taken off LinkedIn after clicking apply

Saving job application answers
Choose if you'd like for LinkedIn to save the information you enter into job applications.

Stored job applicant accounts
Manage which third party job applicant accounts are stored on LinkedIn.

Blocking and hiding

Followers
Choose who can follow you and see your public updates

Blocking
See your list, and make changes if you'd like

Unfollowed
See who you have unfollowed, and resume following if you'd like

As you can see there are many options when it comes to **Privacy**. For the remainder of this topic we'll focus on **Job seeking preferences**. We will discuss **Jobs** in more detail in another chapter. When you are in job search you certainly want to **Let recruiters know you're open to opportunities.** You want to make sure the button in this section is switched to "Yes". This will put you on recruiter's radar for 90 days. NOTE: If you complete the section, Note to recruiters, where you get 300 spaces and characters to market yourself, you need to refresh this every 90 days as LinkedIn deletes this information after that time.

Career interests

Privacy settings

Let recruiters know you're open
We take steps not to show your current company that you're open, but can't guarantee complete privacy. **Learn more**

On

Sharing your profile when you click apply is good to do. Inevitably you're going to be applying to positions on LinkedIn. Having the option to share your LinkedIn profile for the positions you apply to can help you stand out. Remember, your LinkedIn profile is an extension of your resume. It gives you another opportunity to highlight your experience, qualifications, and skills.

Sharing your profile when you click apply

Close

Choose if you want to share your full profile with the job poster when you're taken off LinkedIn after clicking apply

No

Increase your chances of being viewed by sharing your full profile with the job poster when you're taken off LinkedIn to apply

No

You can change the privacy of your photo by selecting the privacy setting you feel most comfortable with. However, making your photo visible to everyone is the best practice if you are actively looking for a job. Photo privacy settings can be found where you uploaded your photo.

Choosing Communications Preferences in the Communications Settings

These settings are worth paying attention to because they control how accessible you are to the LinkedIn community.

Privacy	Communications

Preferences

Notifications on LinkedIn   Change
Manage the alerts you receive in the Notifications tab

Email frequency   Change
Choose what types of emails you wish to receive from LinkedIn

Who can send you invitations   Change
Choose who can send you invitations to connect   Everyone

Messages from members and partners   Change
now what type of messages you'd prefer to receive   inMail

Notifications on LinkedIn is chock full of options to manage the alerts you receive in the **Notifications** Tab. Clicking on the **Notifications on LinkedIn** section will take you to another screen to control options such as:

> Invitations and messages,

> Jobs and opportunities,

> News and articles,

> Updates about you,

> Updates about your network, and

> Updates from your groups.

Each one of these sections has many details you may want to review that you can turn on or off, they all default to "on". LinkedIn has its own set of communications. Review these and set them to match your personal preferences. Whether you have these turned on or off will not affect your job search.

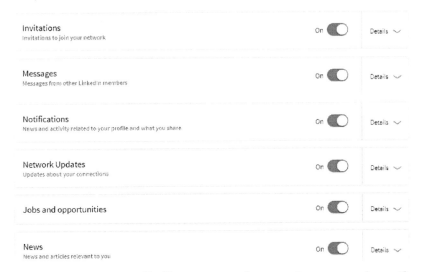

Email frequency will allow you to choose what type of emails you receive from LinkedIn. LinkedIn will send you email to the address you used to register for things like Open Positions, Group Updates, Messages etc. You can select what you want to receive emails for and what you don't. Review each option. If you are in an active job search, select **Individual Email** for each category. This may mean a lot of emails, yet it's the best way to stay in the loop and respond promptly to any opportunities that arise. If you aren't actively looking for work, then you will find the weekly digest or recommended summary option reduces the flow of messages into your inbox. We recommend that you keep the following settings at **Individual Email** for:

➤ Invitations

➤ InMails and Introductions

➤ Messages from your connections

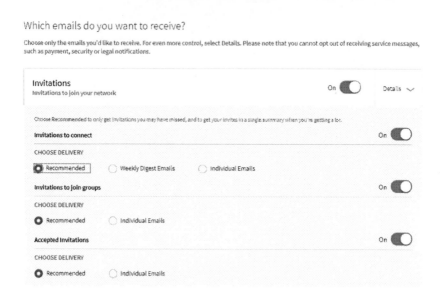

Which emails do you want to receive?

Choose only the emails you'd like to receive. For even more control, select Details. Please note that you cannot opt out of receiving service messages, such as payment, security or legal notifications.

Personalize the remaining settings, recognizing that frequency is good for where you are actively interested in opportunism.

Who can send you invitations is self-explanatory. You could limit it to "Only people who know your email or who appear in your Imported Contacts" or "Only people who appear in your Imported Contacts". You may choose to do this if you don't want just anyone asking to connect with you but you always can just ignore the connection requests that come to you if don't want to connect with them. When you are in a job search, you should definitely allow contacts outside of your network to get in touch with you, so don't change LinkedIn's default "Everyone on LinkedIn".

Messages from members and partners allows you to select the type of messages you're willing to receive. You'll see that LinkedIn defaults to **InMails** and Sponsored **InMails**. Sponsored **InMails** are messages with informational or promotional content from LinkedIn partners.

InMails allow members on LinkedIn who are not connected to you to message you. If they are a premium member they get

InMails as part of their membership. Anyone can **InMail** another LinkedIn user as long as they have a Upgraded account and the person is in their network. This is useful when you have identified someone you'd like to contact but are not connected to them at a 1st degree level. In lieu of getting introduced to them by a common connection you can message them directly by the use of this method. To allow others to **InMail** you, you'll want to be sure the button is switched to "yes".

Below this button you have the option to turn off the ability to all LinkedIn partners to show you Sponsored **InMail**. Sponsored **InMails** are messages with informational or promotional content from LinkedIn partners.

You can't prevent your 1st degree contacts from contacting you but you can always block them.

If you have a Twitter account, you may choose to add it. If so, make sure you use that Twitter account professionally, not to share your personal life. Just like on LinkedIn, keep it professional.

Read Receipts and Typing Indicators

Much like in many email services, you have the option of choosing whether or not you want to send and receive read receipts of the messages you send. You'll be able to see when they are typing in real time but both you and who you're messaging need to have this switched to "yes".

EXPERTS' TIPS

If you do not have any connections in common with your target contact, it's a good idea to identify if that person participates in any online forums you can also join. For example, does he or she use Twitter regularly? You can connect there, share tweets, and engage enough so the person know about you. Or, find out if the contact is active in a LinkedIn group. Once you identify what network the person uses and prefers, you can engage and create a "warm lead."[1]

Without sounding like a broken record, it's very simple to reach out people you've never met. Be curious about them. Before you reach out, consider "what's in it for them?" If you can't think of a reason this person would want connect with you, dig deeper and find one.[2]

---

1   Miriam Salpeter, job search and social networking coach, Keppie Careers (www. keppiecareers.com). Author of 100 Conversations for Career Success (with Laura Labovich) and Social Networking for Career Success.

2   Laura M. Labovich of ASPIRE! EMPOWER! Career Strategy Group (http://aspire-em-power.com/). Author of Two Weeks to Job Search Discovery!

What to Do with Your LinkedIn Profile

You've built your LinkedIn profile. Are you wondering, "Now what?" Status updates and announcements from your personal network will post to your Home page. At a glance, the Notifications section will keep you on top of what's going on with your connections.

To make the most of your interactions on LinkedIn, this is an area to check on regularly. You can respond to individual updates right on your Home page-you can Like, Comment, Reply, or Share updates.

To post your own updates, input messages into the status box and click Post to send message to your network.

What kind of information should you post in your updates?

> Current and upcoming trends in your industry

> Insights from projects you're working on

> Events and seminars you've attended

> Training courses you're taking

> Links to articles/blogs within the industry

> Inspirational quotes

The content that you share doesn't necessarily have to be yours 100 percent of the time. It's a great idea to share links to content from others in your industry, along with your thoughts on how this work will affect your industry.

You can post several updates each day or one every few days. At a minimum, you should post a new update at least once a week.

MAKING CONNECTIONS

L inkedIn organizes your relationships with other LinkedIn members in degrees of separation. This means that people who acknowledge that they know you by connecting with you (1st degree connections) become bridges to additional connections.

There are three levels or degrees outside of your network. 1st degree is assigned to anyone you are directly connected to. 2nd degree is assigned to anyone your direct connections are connected to. 3rd degree is assigned to people who are connected with 2nd degree connections and not a 1st degree connections. The greater the connection level number, the further away from you a connection is.

You can view all 1st degree connections and the number of people you share as connections and their identities.

When you perform a search for people, you'll also see if any of the search results show people connected to you, and at what level.

Knowing what degree a connection is determines your strategy as you work toward growing your network.

Import Contacts

Looking for people one by one wastes valuable time that should be spent on a job search. You could use LinkedIn's search box to locate possible connections, but LinkedIn provides several ways to streamline this process. Once you master these techniques, you'll be ready to move on to connecting with people you don't already know.

For those who use Hotmail, Gmail, AOL, or Yahoo, learning how to import contacts from other email management systems will be a major timesaver. Let's begin by reviewing how to import contacts from one of the main web-based email services.

How to Import Contacts from Hotmail, Gmail, AOL, and Yahoo

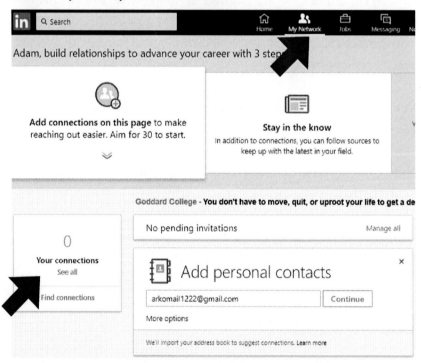

To import contacts, choose the **My Network** menu from the navigation bar. Click **Find connections** on the left side of the page. Then you'll find several choices for importing data.

Whether you decide to have LinkedIn sync with an online email, manually enter contacts yourself, or import from a desktop email, this networking tool makes it simple.

If you have clicked **Find Connections**, you'll see six different options to choose from.

Note: *The Outlook button only works for businesses that allow their employees to log in to their Outlook account remotely. It won't work if you are managing email using Outlook on you home-based business computer.*

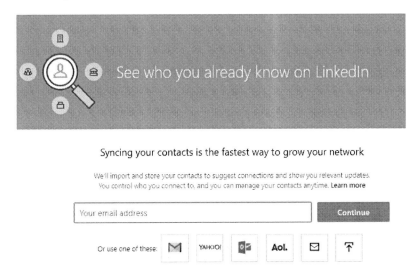

The **Invite by email** option works with many of the common email services around the world.

You will have the opportunity to approve and decline the additions of contacts as LinkedIn searches the designated online email box.

How to Import Contacts from Other Email Applications

You can also upload. CSV, TXT., and VCF files. Most desktop contact management applications – like Outlook – let you export addresses to one of the file types mentioned. You'll find the upload link by clicking on the **Upload a File** icon on the right of the list of email provider choices.

Syncing your contacts is the fastest way to grow your network

We'll import and store your contacts to suggest connections and show you relevant updates. You control who you connect to, and you can manage your contacts anytime. **Learn more**

arkomail1222@gmail.com   Upload a file

Or use one of these: M   YAHOO!   O   Aol.   ✉   ⬆

Of course, you need to create a .CSV, .TXT or .VCF file to upload. I've included the instructions for Outlook below. If you have a different email application, click **Learn More**.

LinkedIn's exact instructions as to how to import your address book are as follows:

Importing your address book

1.   Click the **My Network** icon at the top of your LinkedIn homepage.

2.   Click **See all** below Your connections on the left rail.

3.   Click **Manage synced and imported contacts** on the top of the right rail.

4.   Click **More options** below **Add personal contacts** on the right rail.

5.   Enter your email address in the field or, choose a service provider from the list on the right. If your email provider is not supported, you can still **invite people to connect by email**.

6.   Click **Continue**.

7.   Contacts who are already on LinkedIn will be shown. Click **Add Connections** to send invitations or click **Skip** if you don›t want to invite anyone. Contacts who are not yet on LinkedIn will be displayed next. You may see phone number contacts listed if you›ve imported your mobile contacts previously (these contacts will receive a SMS text invitation to join). Click the Skip link if you don›t want to invite anyone or click **Add to Network** to invite them to join.

Note: LinkedIn states that it will automatically select all contacts on the displayed list to be invited. If you don't want to send invitations to everyone on the list, be sure to uncheck the **Select All** *box and individually check the boxes next to contact you want to invite.*

Once your address file is uploaded, you'll be sent to a page that allows you to choose who you want to ask to connect with you. You don't have to invite everyone in your list. Deselect anyone who isn't someone you have actually worked with or know well.

Email addresses for people who have provided product support, for example, aren't likely to remember you, so an invitation from you might appear to be spam.

Also, does it need to be said? Deselect anyone who you know won't appreciate an invitation from you.

It is also worth checking on the number of contacts the person has as you are making your decisions. A person who has been a member for a year and only has four connections isn't going to be a valuable contact. These individuals have started on a LinkedIn profile, yet aren't willing to put any time into developing their network.

At the same time, if you see someone who can benefit you with a reference, invite them regardless of the number of connections they currently have.

Note: Importing information does not automatically connect you with people. After importing, each person will receive an invite from you to join you network on LinkedIn. Once the recipient accepts the invitation, then you are connected and you will be notified.

When building your presence on LinkedIn, you need to start somewhere. By requesting connections on LinkedIn with people you already know – either in real life or through email correspondence – you can build your network, which will help you realize your job search objectives.

How to Search for Connections

At the top in the black ribbon there is a search bar. To find people, click in the bar and you will see three options: **People, Jobs,** and **Posts.**

You can use this function to identify contacts. You can filter by keywords to search by specific job titles. You can use the variables "Not" and "Or" to define exactly what you are looking for. If you are looking for a local person, or someone who shares certain interests, you can specify this in your search terms.

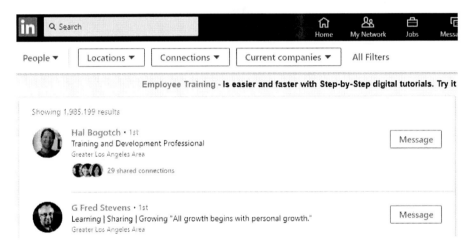

You'll notice that you can search by companies you've worked for, which will help you find former colleagues. You can search by school to find former classmates.

You can also narrow your search by industry. This can be useful if you are searching specifically to grow your network within in you niche.

You can filter your search by only 2nd degree connections. As you will learn later, 2nd degree connections can prove important for gaining exposure within a specific job market. Many times, people connected to your connections can be affiliated with industries / markets that interest you. We'll talk about introductions later.

Ways to Use Search Results

Now that you've found people, how do you connect with them? What do you do with the search results LinkedIn delivers? Regardless of whether you're directly on a profile page or reviewing a listing of profiles from a search, these are the options usually offered to initiate contact:

> Connect

> Send InMail

> Follow

> Get Introduced

> Share Profile

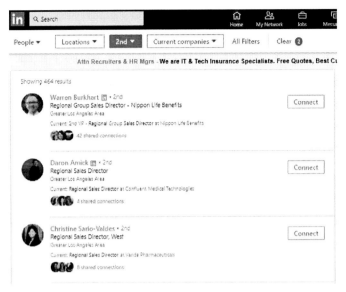

If you move your cursor to the "More" button you'll see a variety of options you can choose. When the person is a 2nd degree or 3rd degree connection, LinkedIn allows you to request a connection directly. Although you should not connect with just anyone you don't know without writing them to explain why you're requesting to connect with them. You can do this with the **Add a note** option that you'll see after you click on **Connect**.

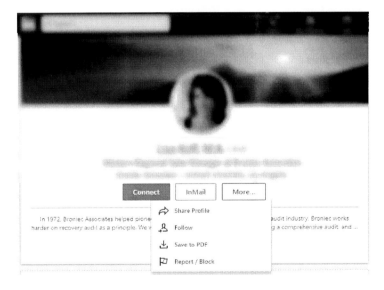

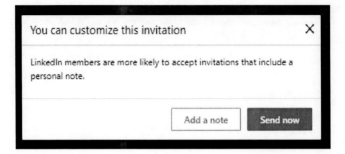

Get Introduced to Make Connections

Getting Introduced is a great option to connect with people you do not already know and would like to know. In this way, someone who knows you is recommending the connection. If you run a search for people for example, with a specific title or at a specific company, LinkedIn will show you how you're connected to these people if you're not already connected. You'll see how many common connections you have with that person.

For example, if you have 7 connections in common that is 7 opportunities you have to reach out to someone you really do know to get introduced to someone you would like to know and who would be strategic for your job search.

The basic idea is that if you don't know a person in which you would like to connect with, find someone within your personal network who can introduce you to this person. When a potential contact sees you are connected to someone he/she knows, it implies you are a credible person.

Take time to write a good explanation for why you are reaching out and why you would like to make the connection. For example:

Hi <name of person>

I hope your work as a PA has been going well. I have been focusing on developing my resume writing skills over the last six months, including adding LinkedIn training to my services.

As I was preparing lesson, I found <name of person I want to connect to > in a search for writer and found that we share a connection. Would you mind introducing me to <first name>? At times, I'm not able to take a client, and I'd like to expand my network with like professionals.

Thanks Fred

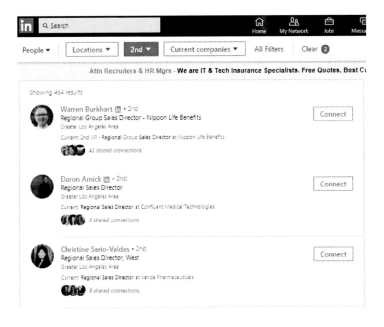

If you have a had a good business relationship with the person who is introducing you, he or she is quite likely to make the introduction gladly. This strategy is good to use when you have a target company and you're trying to make a connection in that target company.

Note if you click on Connect from the search results view, you will not have the opportunity to write a personal note before sending the connection request as you would while viewing the person's LinkedIn profile.

When the person you are interested in connecting with is a 3rd degree connection, you may see the option to **InMail** them. If you have a free membership, you'll have to upgrade to a Premium account in order to send an **InMail** as we discussed earlier.

It's better to get introduced to someone you're not connected to. Think of it as your common connection giving you a warm introduction to someone you don't know versus you cold-calling them.

Share Profile is available to you when you want to recommend a connection between two of your connections. Be very careful about recommending connections between people you don't know and those you do know. Make it very clear that you don't know the person you are recommending.

For example, if a writer was too busy to take on a project for a contact, a person might recommend that the person check out the qualifications of another writer with an impressive profile.

How to Use Connect

In general, when a person is a 3rd degree connection in your network, it isn't worth cold connecting. It's too easy to be labeled a spammer. Nevertheless, if you share a common career path, it can be a good strategy to grow your connections through carefully written invitations.

For example, perhaps the 3rd degree professional is someone you have spoken with on a conference call or webinar or communicated with via email. This individual may not use the same email on LinkedIn as you have in your list. This would be an ideal person to reach out to and ask for a connection. In this scenario, it makes the most sense to click **Connect.**

The key to remember is this: don't assume the person will remember you. Trigger his or her memory with something that will create a connection. Personalize the message; It will pay off in more connections.

More about Using InMails to Connect

We discuss using **InMails** several times because they can play an important role in your job search strategy. As mentioned earlier, **InMails** are a paid feature of LinkedIn that enable you to send emails directly to a person's LinkedIn mailbox, regardless of whether or not they're in your network. You have to have a premium (paid) account in order to send **InMails**. Depending on your premium account level, you'll receive a credit for a certain number of **InMails** per month. You can receive **InMails** with a free account, but not send them.

Although **InMails** require payment – and you're running a risk by contacting someone who doesn't know you personally – they can be an effective way to connect with someone who you don't know directly. Using **InMails** to meet a fellow LinkedIn member shows you're serious about your search and willing to invest to make the right connections.

Messages

When you are already connected to the person, you will have different options than when they are not part of your network. The primary option that changes is the ability to message on LinkedIn. This service is free.

STRATEGY TIP

Indicate that you like an update. Leave a comment. These are discrete ways to gain the attention of people in your network who may be hard to connect with otherwise.

How to Make Inroads with Invites

Technically, you can send a LinkedIn invite at any time. You just click **Connect** beside any search result. With the **Connect** feature, you don't need a connection or a paid account. However, use discretion with this method. Recipients can respond by stating they don't know you and preventing you from sending another connection request. If you receive too many "I don't know this person" responses, LinkedIn may restrict you from sending invitations altogether.

Always change the default text when inviting someone to connect. The default phrase is, "I'd like to add you to my professional network on LinkedIn." Change this to highlight a personal connection instead. For example, "I enjoyed meeting you at the workshop yesterday. I'd like to connect with you on LinkedIn to keep in touch."

Take Action!

Follow the steps given to import your existing contacts into LinkedIn. Then, use the **Search** function discussed in this chapter to see who else pops up that you can connect with. Next, run and **Create a search alert**.

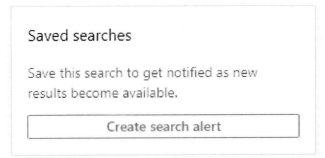

Post a status update after you have completed these instructions.

Plan on posting at least one status update each day this week by doing something from this or one of the previous lessons that you want to share.

REFERENCES FOR BUILDING CREDIBILITY

References are a powerful tool in a job search. Recommendations on LinkedIn serve much the same purpose. A recommendation is "social proof" from a third party that you're a skilled professional.

According to LinkedIn, "Users with recommendations in their profiles are three times more likely to receive relevant offers and inquiries through searches on LinkedIn."

In fact, if LinkedIn is still telling you that your profile isn't quite complete, this could be the primary reason.

LinkedIn recommendations are a natural evolution of references and letters of recommendation. However, they often are more credible than these traditional documents because it is harder to fake a recommendation on LinkedIn than it is to forge a letter. Since many companies are restricting reference checks to verification of title and dates of employment, a LinkedIn recommendation from a supervisor-and/or coworkers-carries weight.

Many describe LinkedIn as a "reputation engine." That's an apt description because your reputation does precede you online – not just in your work history, but also in your LinkedIn recommendations.

Someone looking at your recommendations wants to know two things:

> What are you like?

> Are you good at what you do?

In addition, you can enhance you own reputation by providing recommendations because people viewing your profile can see (and read) the recommendations you make.

Recommendations provide Search Engine Optimization (SEO) results – meaning, they help you get noticed – both on LinkedIn, as well as search engines. Use industry-specific terminology in your recommendations. Keywords included in LinkedIn recommendations also receive emphasis in search engine results – especially searches within LinkedIn. When conducting a keyword search, all keywords in a profile are indexed, and profiles with a high match of relevant keywords rank higher in search listings. Although LinkedIn's specific algorithms are secret, some experts suggest that keywords in recommendations receive double the rankings of keywords provided in the profile itself.

Building Your Recommendation Base

Recommendations are visible to your personal network and Fortune 500 companies utilizing the LinkedIn Recruiter Tool. They are important primarily because of the perception that they are very difficult to falsify. These recommendations could be one of the factors that land you the job.

How many recommendations you should have on your profile depends on how many contacts you have. A good guideline is 1-2 recommendation for every 50 connections. Ideally, these will be a variety of individuals – not just supervisors, but co-workers, people you supervise, and clients/customers. Choose quality over quantity.

Plan to build your recommendation over time. Because recommendation have a date attached to them, don't try to solicit all of your recommendations at once. Don't write and send your recommendations all at once either. Recommendations are date-stamped, so the reader will be able to see when she or he was added to your page. It's best if they are added over time.

All recommendations now have their own section called "Recommendations" which is now located under the "Skills and Endorsements" section discussed earlier.

The Recommendations Process

The simplest way to get recommendations is to ask for one. To request a recommendation through LinkedIn, click the **More** button on the person's profile and you will see the option to request a recommendation.

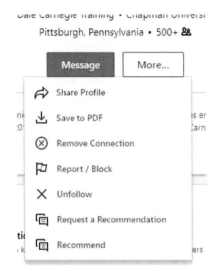

You'll be taken to a page where LinkedIn asks you to complete how you know them and the position at the time of the person you wish to recommend.

Click next and LinkedIn will take you to the next screen where you will compose a message to the person you're asking a recommendation from.

LinkedIn provides a generic message. It is recommended that you personalize the message. For example, you could choose to get recommended by connections that worked with you on a specific type of project. Then ask that set of connections to endorse your work for that project. Each request should be personalized to the individual you are a recommendation from.

For example:

"Could you provide me with a recommendation based on our work together on [X Project]?"

You sample request might look like this:

"Could you provide me with a recommendation based on our work together on your resume? I am developing my LinkedIn profile for this service, and your feedback on the quality of my work would be helpful!

Thanks!

Andrew"

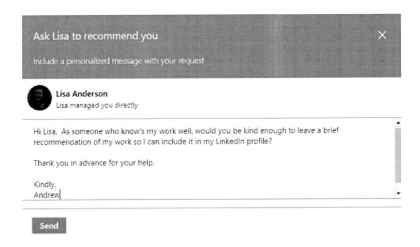

Another alternative:

"Hi <name> is a lot more personal and more likely to receive a response.

Ultimately, the best strategy is to ask for the recommendation through more personal means – for example, in person, on the telephone, or via email.

In fact, one of the best ways to get a LinkedIn recommendation is to ask after they've given you a compliment in real life. If they praise you via email, for example, you could respond with a message that thanks them and says, "Are you on LinkedIn? Would you mind if I sent you a LinkedIn request for a recommendation? It would mean a lot to me to have you say that in a recommendation on there."

Reciprocation is also a powerful motivation for recommendations. Generally, if you ask someone for a recommendation, she or he will expect you to write one for them. (So, it's a good idea to only ask for recommendations from someone you'd be willing to write one for in return!) The reverse is also true – sometimes, if you provide an unsolicited recommendation, the person you recommend is likely to write one for you, as well.

However, reciprocal recommendations (I gave you one, so can you give me one?) are less powerful than recommendations that are freely given. Remember, visitors to your LinkedIn profile can see who you have recommended as well as who has recommended you. It's easy to spot one-to-one (reciprocal) recommendations.

If you don't receive a response back from someone after requesting a recommendation – or, if you don't feel comfortable following up, consider whether you should be asking for a recommendation from that person in the first place.

One of the most effective ways to get a great LinkedIn recommendation is to write it yourself. This makes it easier on the person who you want to recommend you – and ensures your recommendation is specific and detailed.

In this case, your request for a recommendation might follow this format:

Dear (Name):

I'm writing to request a recommendation of our work together at (company name) that I can included on my LinkedIn profile. To make this easy for you, here's a draft recommendation. Feel free to edit this or create your own.

Thank you,

(Your Name)

When possible, give the person you're asking for a recommendation some context for your request:

"I'm writing you to request a recommendation on LinkedIn. As you know, I'm looking to make a career change, and I believe a recommendation from you based on our work together on [X Project] would be useful in highlighting my transferable skills."

How to Handle Recommendations

You'll receive a notification when someone recommends you. LinkedIn sends the notification to the email address on file. The link at the bottom of the email takes you to the same message in your LinkedIn account (you may need to sign in to your LinkedIn account). It will ask you if you want to "Show this recommendation on my profile." Choose one option and then click Accept recommendation.

After you click Accept recommendation, you'll receive a Recommendation Confirmation.

If you find an error in your recommendation or it's not specific enough, you can click the Ask for revision button and it will automatically generate a request for a change with an email to the individual who wrote the recommendation.

The best way to handle a recommendation that you don't like is simply to ask for it to be revised. Instead of asking them to change the whole thing, address specific issues in the recommendation that you would like changed.

"I like what you've written, but I was wondering if you would correct the statement where you said I brought in $200,000 in revenue; my records from that time show that the figure was closer to $375,000."

Replace the standard text in the message with your custom message.

STRATEGY TIP

Asking for changes in a recommendation should be handled carefully. Here are some tips that may prevent misunderstandings:

- Correct any spelling and/or punctuation errors. Ask if the corrected version could be used.

- Copy some quotes from your contact's emails. Ask if this information could be included in the recommendation.

- Ask your contact to share what he/she liked the most about working with you and what he/she would want others to know about you.

Removing Recommendations

You can also choose to not show recommendations from your profile, even after it is published. Here is how to manage the recommendations already on your LinkedIn profile: From your profile view scroll down to the **Recommendations** section. You will see what looks like this:

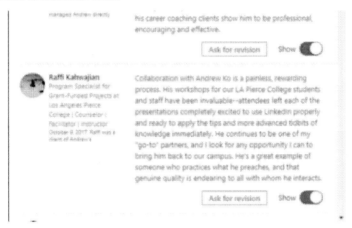

LinkedIn displays each recommendation. By clicking the pencil icon, LinkedIn will take you into **Manage recommendations** where you can **Ask for revisions** on each one or choose to show or not show them.

What to Do with Poor Recommendations

You can also refuse recommendations. When you receive a message notifying you of a recommendation, if it is not a good one, you can choose not to show it on your profile.

There are several reasons you might wish to do this. Perhaps whomever wrote the recommendation isn't a strong writer.

If you prefer not to **Ask for a revision**, you could edit the recommendation for grammar and punctuation and ask your connection to update their recommendation with your revised text.

It is preferable if you have a good working relationship to use the **Ask for revision** option. You may have coworkers who have weak writing skills, yet would contribute value to your profile with their recommendation if they receive a bit of help from you.

Leaving Recommendations

If you provide recommendations (especially for previous and current colleagues), they are likely to reciprocate, so spend some time crafting thoughtful, unique recommendations for people you know.

Formula for Writing LinkedIn Recommendations

Before you write anything, look at your contact's LinkedIn profile. Align your recommendation with the individual's LinkedIn profile.

Tie in what you write with their headline, summary, and/or experience – reinforce the qualities they want to emphasize in the recommendation you write.

Look at the existing recommendations they've received, as well.

Some things to consider in your recommendation include:

➤ What are they good at doing?

➤ What did they do better than anyone else did?

➤ What impact did they have on me? (How did they make my life better/easier?)

➤ What made them stand out?

➤ Is there a specific result they delivered in the position?

➤ What surprised you about the individual?

Choose the qualities you want to emphasis in the person you are recommending.

You may choose to use what author and speaker Lisa B. Marshall calls "The Rule of Threes." Simply stated, concepts or ideas presented in groups of three are more interesting, more enjoyable, and more memorable.

In general, you will want to showcase transferable skills, because these will be the most relevant for your contacts when they are using LinkedIn for a job search or business development tool.

Recommendations and Endorsements

In 2013, LinkedIn introduced the "endorsement"—a vague and essentially worthless way to tell others what someone in your network knows how to do well. Endorsements make connections feel like they've helped someone in their network. Unfortunately, endorsements don't carry any weight.

Only recommendations carry any real value on LinkedIn. This is one major reason you need to pursue them.

If your request is ignored, there are several strategies to consider.

1. Make it easy for connections by providing a template. Your connection may not feel comfortable with writing recommendations.

2. Your connections may have forgotten. A reminder is easy to send. Go to Manage Your Recommendations, click Resend, and edit the message so it's a friendly reminder.

3. If your connection's memories aren't as positive as you anticipated, withdraw the request.

The following formula for a LinkedIn recommendation will help you write a great recommendation.

➤ Start with how you know the person (1 sentence). Give context for the relationship beyond just the job title and organization/company/school, although that can be a good way to start your recommendation. ("I've known Amy for 10 years, ever since I joined XYZ Company. She was my lead project manager when I was an analyst.")

➤ Be specific about why you are recommending the individual (1 sentence). What qualities make him or her most valuable? Emphasize what the person did that set him or her apart. What is his work style? Does she have a defining characteristic? To be effective, recommendations should focus on specific qualifications.

➤ Tell a story (3-5 sentences). Back up your recommendation with a specific example. Your recommendation should demonstrate that you know the person well – so tell a story that only you could tell. Moreover, provide social proof in the story – give scope for the accomplishments. Don't just say the individual you're recommending led the team – say he led a 5-person team or a 22-person team. Supporting evidence – numbers, percentages, and dollar figures – lends detail and credibility to your story.

➤ End with a call to action (1 sentence). Finish with the statement, "I recommend (name)" and the reason why you would recommend him or her.

In the first sentence, you described how you know the individual and give context about why you are qualified to recommend him or her.

➤ (name) and I have worked together ...

➤ I've known (name) for (how long) ...

For the second bullet point, you can set up the description of his or her qualities by providing an overview sentence.

Here are some examples:

➤ Able to delegate...

➤ Able to implement...

➤ Able to plan...

- Able to train...

- Consistent record of...

- Customer-centered leader...

- Effective in_____

- Experienced professional in the _____ industry

- Held key role in _____

- Highly organized and effective...

- High-tech achiever recognized for ...

- Proficient in managing multiple priorities and projects ...

- Recognized and appreciated by...

- Served as a liaison between _____

- Strong project manager with ...

- Subject-matter expert in _____

- Team player with...

- Technically proficient in _____

- Thrived in an ...

- Valued by clients and colleagues for ...

- Well-versed in the...

For example:

Mike had a consistent record of delivering year-over-year sales revenue increases while also ensuring top-notch customer service, working effectively with the entire 7-member sales team to make sure the client's needs were met.

Jill is a subject-matter expert in logistics, warehouse planning, and team leadership. Her ability to take the initiative to ensure the prioritization of thousands of items in each shipment for same-day processing made her an indispensable member of the management team.

For the storytelling section, you can choose a **Challenge-Action-Result** (CAR) format to describe the project:

> **Challenge**: What was the context for the work situation on the project? What was the problem that the project was designed to tackle?

> **Action**: What did the person you're recommending do? What was their specific contribution?

> **Result**: What was the outcome of the project-and can you quantify it?

Choose descriptive adjectives to include in your recommendations. Instead of describing someone as innovative" choose a word like "forward-thinking" or "pioneering."

Make sure the recommendation you write is clearly about the person you're recommending. That sounds like common sense, but many recommendations are too vague or too general – they could be about anyone, not this specific individual. To be effective, the recommendation you write should not be applicable to anyone else.

Recommendations that you write should be:

> Genuine

> Specific

> Descriptive (with detailed characteristics)

> Powerful (including specific achievements, when possible)

> Honest/Truthful (credibly is important; avoid puffery or exaggeration)

Length is an important consideration when writing LinkedIn recommendations. Keep your recommendations under 200 words whenever possible. Some of the most effective LinkedIn recommendations are only 50-100 words.

You may find it useful to look at other recommendations before writing yours. You can do a search on LinkedIn for others with that job title and check out the recommendations.

Now you're ready to actually create a recommendation using LinkedIn.

The easiest way to do this is to go to the profile of the person you want to recommend. Click the **More** button and select the appropriate option.

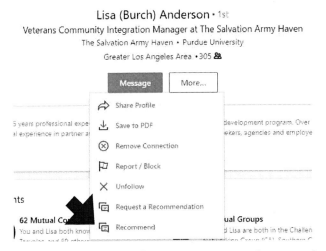

You then will follow a similar process as we discussed when requesting a recommendation by selecting their relationship to you and their title at the time. Click **Next** and write the recommendation following the tips we've discussed.

The person you recommend will get an email notifying him or her that you've made a recommendation. If you don't receive a reply from the individual you've recommended within a week, follow up and make sure they received it.

Keep in mind that you can change (or remove) recommendations you've given. To do this scroll down to Recommendations while on your profile. Follow the instructions outlined in the previous page to hide the visibility of a recommendation, if necessary. Click **Given** and then click the **pencil icon** to the right of the section.

Recommendations

Ask to be recommended

Received (25)   Given (19)

5 recommendation requests

Raffi Kahwaiian

You can edit recommendations from this section by clicking on **Revise.**

Responding to Recommendation Requests

Don't ignore request for recommendations. But don't feel as if you must accept all requests to make a recommendation. You can respond back that you don't feel you know him or her well enough to write a recommendation (or that you don't know them well enough in their work life to recommend them, if you only know them socially). Alternatively, you can put them off by saying, "Once we've worked together for a while, I'd be happy to write a recommendation for you."

So-called "character references" (also called "personal references") don't have much of a place on LinkedIn, where the emphasis is on recommendations from people you have worked with ("professional references"). You can say something like, "Although we know each other socially, because LinkedIn attaches recommendations to specific jobs, I don't feel I'm a good fit to write a recommendation for you."

You will rarely see negative recommendation on LinkedIn. Because the content of recommendations is public, it's likely to be positive, and since recipients can choose to display recommendations or not, they are not likely to approve negative comments for public display.

Your mom was right: "If you can't say anything nice, don't say anything at all."

However, if you do decide to write a recommendation, the first question you should ask is "What is the goal?" Does the individual want a new job? A promotion? A career change? A client? Knowing what their goal is in soliciting a recommendation will help you tailor it to meet their needs.

Look at the individual's LinkedIn profile – especially the job description of the position when you worked together.

If asked to provide a recommendation, it is acceptable to ask the person to draft the recommendation in which you can refine.

Remember, recommendations you write show up on your profile too, so someone looking at your profile can see the recommendation you've made for others.

Final Thoughts on Recommendations

Recommendations matter – but who they came from is sometimes more important than what the recommendation says. A recommendation from a higher-level person makes more of an impact than one from colleagues.

Don't write – or display bad recommendations on your LinkedIn profile. Bad recommendations are those that are:

> Generic

> From people who don't have a clear understanding of you and/or your work

> Written without context (doesn't include how they know you, how they worked with you)

> Old or outdated

POWER TIP

According to LinkedIn expert David Lanners, keywords that appear in Recommendations on LinkedIn count twice when calculating search engine results.

Take Action!

On LinkedIn, it's always best to remember that those who give are those that receive. Make "Give to Get" your motto for this week. Take the time to craft 4-6 well thought-out recommendations for your connections this week, and watch for the reciprocating response.

FINDING JOBS THROUGH COMPANY SEARCHES

F inding a job is more than finding an employer who will hire you. It's finding a position that's a good fit for you and the company for which you end up working. One of LinkedIn's most powerful functions is the insight it provides into various companies and the jobs they offer.

One of the most obvious applications for using LinkedIn in your job search is using the Jobs tab to identify opportunities. Click Jobs in the main navigation bar.

This takes you to the main job search page. By default, the jobs that you'll see on the page are recommendations based upon the keywords you have used in your profile. This is a just a start. You'll want to drill down to find more opportunities.

*Note: You may see a message at the bottom of the search results asking you to **Complete your profile to see improved job suggestions.** If the only obstacle between you and a complete profile is the number of contacts, consider how many requests you have sent out. If you have sent out a large number of requests recently, please give people a week to respond. LinkedIn will send out reminders to people you've asked for connections, so you don't have to become a pest!*

LinkedIn search has changed a lot throughout the years and will most likely continue to change. Even as I'm writing this book, LinkedIn made changes to its layout. If you enter a specific search in the **Search Jobs** box and run a search, you will get results from that keyword search and geographic area. In order to get the broadest results, avoid putting keywords in quotes. If you are only interested in a narrower section of the market, using quotes around your keyword phrase can reduce the number of off-target results.

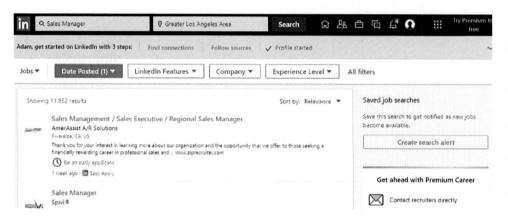

You can identify positions by job title, keywords, or company. **Search** filters appear by clicking on Search on the right side, clicking on the magnifying glass on the left side, or after you have run an initial search.

Expand your filters menu by clicking **All Filters**. With a basic free account, you can filter by: Date posted, LinkedIn Features, Job Type, Location, Company, Industry, Job Function, and Experience Level.

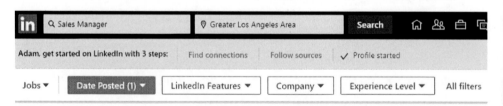

While you are reviewing job matches, you'll notice that you will have the option to **Save it**. If you are interested in the position, click **Save** to add it to your **Saved Jobs** area. After you've completed your search for the day, you can then visit the **Saved Jobs** area to review all the positions that interest you.

You'll notice that to the right of your search results, there's a **Create search alert** button. Click there if you want to create searches that you can save and have emailed to you daily, weekly, or monthly.

If you click the job title, it will take you to the Job Description. Some job postings allow you to apply for the position directly from the page with a feature called "**Easy Apply**", whereas other postings will take you to the company's website.

On the right side of this page, you will see an area called **People Also Viewed** with links to others similar jobs.

There is one thing you should keep your eye out for when you see a job posting. You should watch for jobs where someone on LinkedIn is in your network. In the listing below, you can see that there is a 1st degree connection that could refer you to the company.

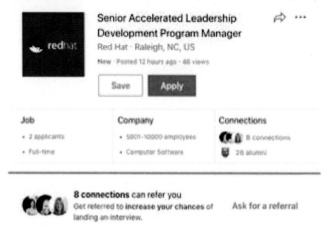

Approximately 50 percent of the job postings will also show you who posted the job.

In some cases, you can send the job poster an InMail and let them know that you applied for the job and would love to have a conversation about how you are a great fit.

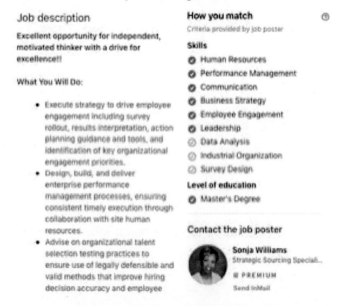

Conducting Company Searches

You can also research companies on LinkedIn and it is wise to do so. Click the magnifying glass in the search bar the top of your screen to get to the search view. Click on **More**, then click on companies. There are over 9,000,000 companies on LinkedIn.

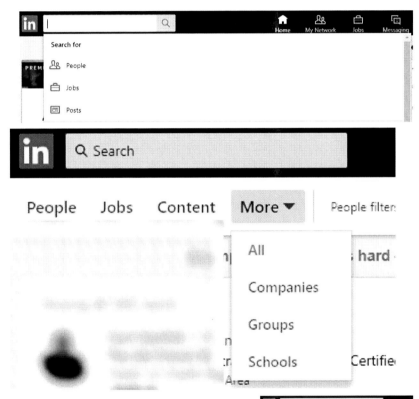

You don't have to know a company name to perform a company search. Use keywords to find companies that meet your interests. LinkedIn will make suggestions automatically. You can click on any of these or simply hit

enter to review the search results for companies using the keyword of "sales".

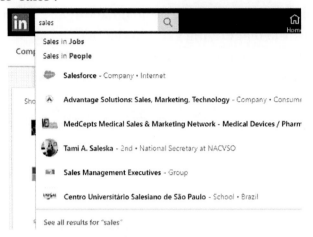

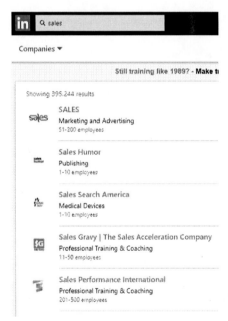

Clicking on the company name will take you to their company page on LinkedIn where you can view all of their details. LinkedIn doesn't give you the option to save your search, so it's a good practice to hold down the CTRL key when you click. This will open the company page in a new window. That way you can explore the company's LinkedIn information without losing your search.

A company's page on LinkedIn is full of useful information on that company. The most useful from a job search perspective is the **See jobs** button. Clicking this will provide a list of their open positions they have posted on LinkedIn. In addition to finding job postings, you may find the profiles of people who work at that company, you'll be able to see if any of your 1st degree connections work there, and you'll see if anyone from your school was hired there.

Don't overlook the information you find on a company's page. They may have information that could be a major resource for you. For example, doing a company search for resume writers could lead you to their company page where you see their recent post that would give you insights into "Best practices on countering a counter offer." Knowing this information could give you the edge in when negotiating for salary and other benefits. In addition to seeing recent posts from the company you'll see company details such as: their website, where they are headquartered, year founded, company size and more. You'll also see what **Groups** on LinkedIn they are affiliated with and the size of that Group. We'll talk more about Groups later.

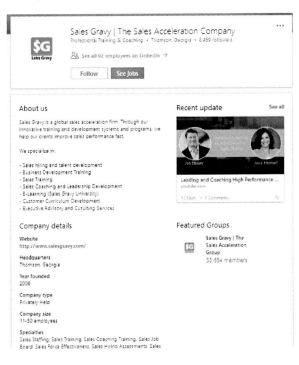

We can take a look a LinkedIn's company page and not surprisingly they offer a lot of information. In addition to the features we discussed previously, LinkedIn's company page also includes a Life section. Here, you can learn more about the company leadership, its products, and its culture. We can also see that at the time of writing this LinkedIn has 15,301 employees on LinkedIn, 12 from our school were hired here, and if we had any 1st degree connections at this company we would see them here.

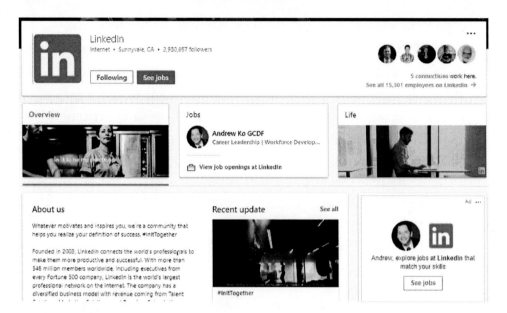

Follow Companies

You can use the **Follow** feature to track prospective employers. When you follow a company, you'll get notices of major changes and notifications when the company loses, gains, or promotes staff (which can be useful to see which companies have a lot of turn over.

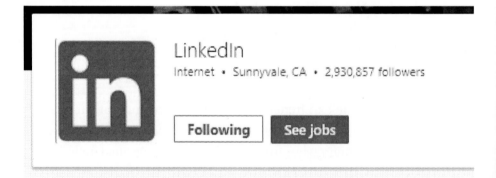

To follow a company, first find the company using the search feature. You will see the option to **Follow** the company in both the search results and on the company's page.

You'll be able to access a list of the companies you follow from your profile page and scrolling down to your "Interests" located at the bottom of your profile. Click on **See all.** You'll see four categories of whom you're following: **Influencers, Companies, Groups,** and **Schools.** Click on **Companies** and you will see a check mark and "Following" next to it. Click it to **Unfollow** the company if you choose to do so.

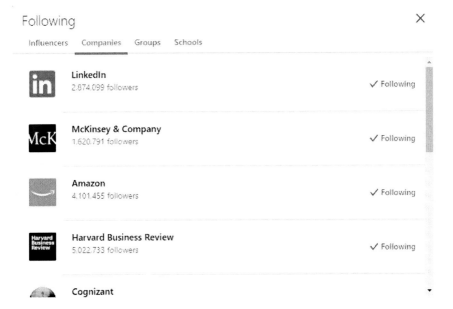

Take Action!

Use the Jobs tab to identity job openings, but don't stop there. Identify 2-3 companies that you'd like to work for which have openings.

Search those companies on LinkedIn to learn more about them. Follow these companies, and use Insightful Statistics data to connect more fully.

THE POWER OF GROUPS

J oining a LinkedIn Group provides you with opportunities to strengthen connections with like-minded individuals in an exclusive forum setting. The **Groups** function provides a private space to interact with LinkedIn members who share common skills, experiences, industry affiliations, and goals. You can easily find groups within your industry to join, as well as local groups.

Laura DeCarlo's Critical 3-Part LinkedIn Strategy

1. Complete your profile in full.

2. Reach out to colleagues, coworkers, and bosses and give them recommendations before you expect them to be written for you.

3. Become an ACTIVE member in as many relevant groups for your profession and industry, as possible.

These easy steps will allow you to: a) make contacts in your sphere, b) improve your search-ability, and c) make your presence value-added.

Laura DeCarlo, President of Career Directors International – **www. careerdirectors.com**.

You may view your **Groups** you're currently in by clicking on **Work** in the top black ribbon portion of **LinkedIn** and then **Groups** from the new window or you may search for groups by using keywords or a group name by clicking the magnifying glass in the search field at the top and clicking More and then Groups in the dropdown.

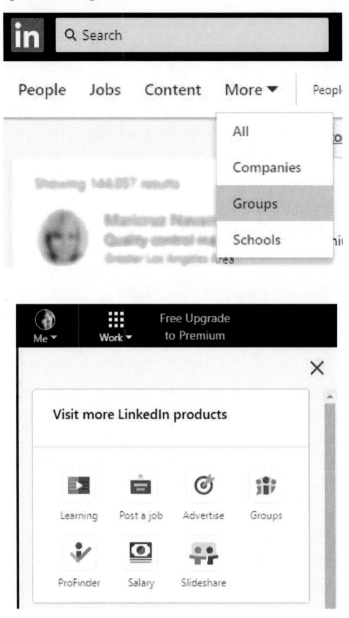

Click the search field the top of the page and use keywords to find groups you may be interested in.

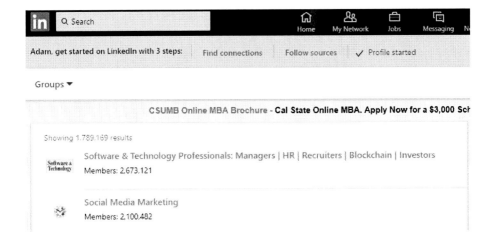

There are over 2,000,000 Groups on LinkedIn, this number includes the two types of Groups: Standard Groups and Unlisted Groups. Anyone can request to join a Standard Group. Unlisted Groups are not searchable by any search engine which means you won't see them when searching for groups to join and one can only join an Unlisted Group by invitation by the Group owner or admin or by requesting to join if they have the URL. If the group is a Closed group (such as university alumni, it may be listed, however your request to join may be denied if you are not an official member of that association.

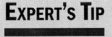

EXPERT'S TIP

Groups can be a very good way to get to know people in your field if it is an active group.[1]

---

1   Miriam Salpeter, job search and social networking coach, Keppie Careers (www.keppiecareers.com). Author of 100 Conversations for Career Success (with Laura Labovich) and Social Networking for Career Success.

Searching for a Group focused in the sales industry using a keyword of "sales" results in (at the time of writing this) 19,814 results.

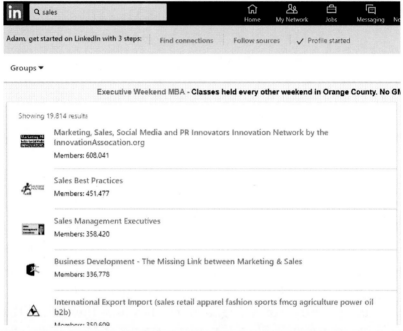

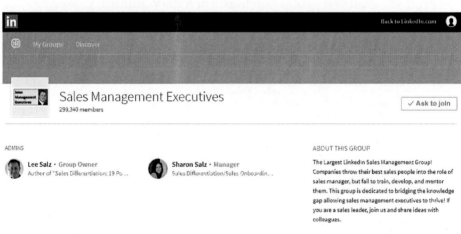

In this example we can see how many members the Groups have and clicking on the title of the Group will take you to the Group where you can **Ask to join** and read more information about the Group.

Note: Your request to join a Group may not be approved immediately.

You'll notice that this search produced a list of groups for someone who wants to develop his or her credibility in the career services industry. Apply this same principle to your search for groups. Narrow your choices by using industry and career-focused keywords.

If we select the Group in the second row we will see more detailed information such as how many members are in the Group, an "About This Group" section, and who of your current 1st degree connections are currently members of the Group. If you see that there are many of your peers from your industry in the group there is a good chance it's a group you might consider joining yourself.

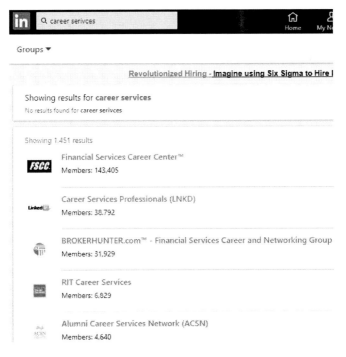

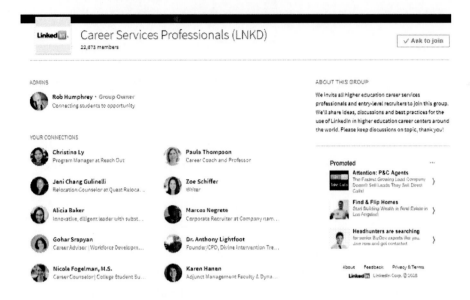

An important benefit and strategy when it comes to Groups is the ability to message the members of the Group even if they are not a 1st degree connection. As discussed earlier in this book, you cannot message people directly if you are not connected to them. Unless of course you are a Premium member and use an InMail. By using Groups, you can message its members because you are both members. It's a good practice once you've been accepted into a Group to take a look at its members and see who you could reach out to.

As we see here in this example, I could directly message this fellow Group member who happens to be the Director of HR of a large well-known company even though I'm not connected to her.

Groups You May Like

Because the number of Groups is so high, LinkedIn also suggests Groups you may be interested in joining. You can access this feature by clicking on **Work** in the top black ribbon portion of **LinkedIn** and then **Groups** from the new window.

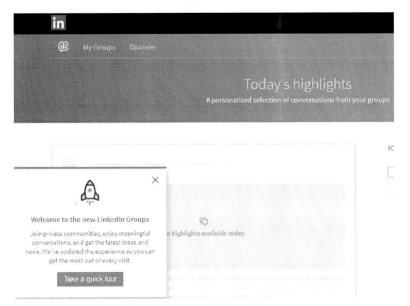

You have the choice clicking on **My Groups** or Discover. My Groups will take you the Groups you're already a member of and the Groups that you manage. By clicking on **Discover**, LinkedIn will suggest Groups for you based on the information you provided in your profile, and they are usually related to your industry.

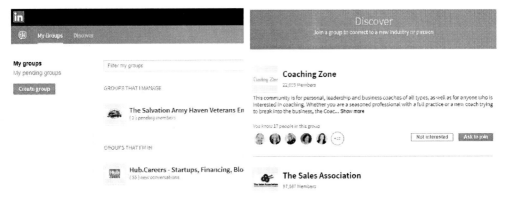

You can manage all of your Groups in the **My Groups** section. You can choose to leave groups if you wish and control the amount of notifications and messages you receive.

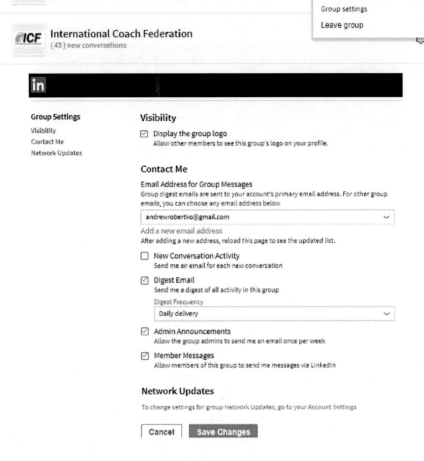

Checklist for Maximizing Your Use of Groups

Click on the Groups tab to:

- Review groups you're currently a member of, if any.

- Search for "Groups You May Like" based on primary keywords, categories, languages, or similar groups within the same interests.

- Check the Groups Directory for featured groups in your niche or areas of interest you might like to join.

- Create a Group of your own to attract followers, entering a logo, group name, type, brief and full description, website, and email address as well as access option, language, and location.

If you are joining a group to develop relationships with influencers, participate in the group to gain visibility before you invite them to connect you on LinkedIn. To establish a presence, ask questions, give advice, and be helpful to others. You can have group notifications emailed to you.

Groups with the largest number of members aren't always the best groups in which to participate. Some Groups require a high standard from members, and thus the number of members remains lower. Don't let this dissuade you from considering the group. Some of the best rest among of very small, yet selective groups.

Should I start a group? Or is it better to start a Discussion in a Group?

Answers from the Experts

- If you have the time and energy for a new group, and you have the follow-through to expand and grow the group, it can be a great way to demonstrate leadership in your field. However, if there is already an active group relevant to your expertise, it can useful to become an active participant and influencer.

- It's easiest to start a Discussion in an existing Group that already has an audience. Owning a group is powerful, but most job seekers want immediate results. Starting your own Group will have long-term benefits, but you might not see those benefits as soon as you need them.

LEVERAGING THE POWER OF MEDIA

Rich Media

L inkedIn offers the ability to add Rich Media. There is a media button in the following sections: Summary, Education, and Experience.

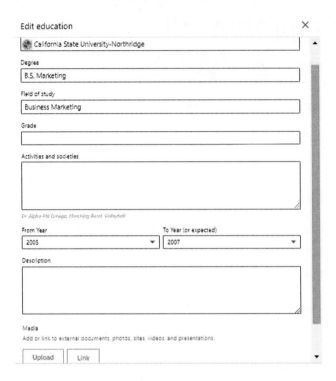

LinkedIn allows you to add videos, images, documents, and presentations directly to your profile. The following file formats that can be uploaded:

Video

> .MOV

> .WMV

> .MP4

Images

> Adobe PDF (.pdf)

> Microsoft PowerPoint (.ppt/.pps/.pptx/.ppsx/.pot/.potx)

> Microsoft Word (.doc/.docx/.rtf)

➤ OpenOffice Presentation Document (.odp)

➤ OpenOffice Documents (.odt)

➤ Most .txt files

➤ .jpg/.jpeg

➤ .png

➤ .bmp

➤ .gif – this doesn't support animation, however the first frame will be extracted

➤ .tiff

Infographics

➤ Adobe PDF (.pdf)

Presentations

➤ Adobe PDF (.pdf)

➤ OpenOffice Presentation Document (.odp)

➤ Microsoft PowerPoint (.ppt/ .pps/ pptx/ .pot/ potx)

Documents

➤ Adobe PDF (.pdf)

➤ Microsoft Word (.doc/ .docx/ .rft)

➤ OpenOffice Documents (.odt)

➤ Most .txt files

SlideShare

SlideShare allows you to upload and share your presentations with millions of professionals around the world. Your presentations can be shared across LinkedIn, Twitter, Facebook. You can also upload your presentation into your profile with the rest of you Rich Media.

To use SlideShare, go to **www.slideshare.net**

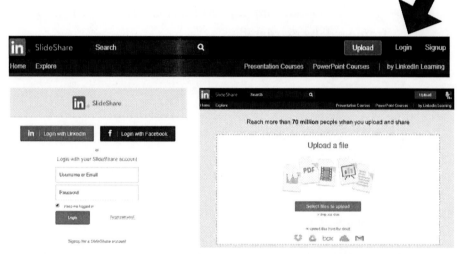

To upload a presentation, click **Upload**. You will then select the appropriate file to upload. While it's uploading, type in the title, a description of the presentation, what category it should be in, whether or not you wish to make it Public, and select "Tag" to help make your presentation discoverable. The more information you provide the higher your "Discoverability Score" will be.

Once uploaded you can control the visibility of your presentation or slideshow and choose if you want to make it downloadable. Share your SlideShare for increased visibility or you can choose to upload it to your profile by using the link like in the example above.

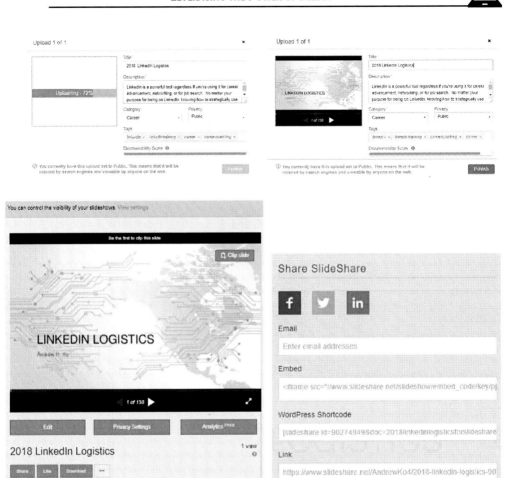

Use the **Link** button next to the **Upload** button in your Summary edit view to use the link the SlideShare provides and link it to your profile as Rich Media.

When you're done, your profile could look something like this.

FINAL THOUGHTS

If you've been taking action, as recommended, you've already:

> Created a LinkedIn account

> Optimized your LinkedIn profile (including a photo, headline, and summary)

> Set your LinkedIn privacy settings

> Made connections with people you know

> Researched (and followed) companies you'd like to work for

> Joined a number of LinkedIn Groups

> Requested and received recommendations to complete you profile

However, to get the most out of LinkedIn – especially for your job search – you need to make LinkedIn a regular part of your routine.

If you're in an active job search, your routine should include logging in to LinkedIn each day to:

> Update your status

> Make new connections

➤ Research employers

➤ Read – and start – threads in your LinkedIn Groups

➤ Give recommendations to your connections

Now, here are some additional strategies you can use to uncover hidden opportunities.

Nurture Local Connections

Search LinkedIn for business and potential contacts using a keyword search. Much of your job search strategy focuses on developing a person-to-person network, and LinkedIn is a good place to find out whom you need to connect with in person. Then, you can uncover who you know that can help you meet the right people via LinkedIn.

That's a first step toward meeting in person for an informational interview, a very useful strategy for any job seeker who is finding it difficult to locate openings to which he or she may apply.

Another opportunity you should look into on LinkedIn is volunteer openings at local non-profits. Filling a time of unemployment with volunteer activities looks good on your LinkedIn profile. It helps dispel the perception that you are unemployable especially when your job search is within one of the sectors that has experienced a downturn in recent years.

Leverage More Out of Company Information

As you are looking through the information a company has posted on LinkedIn, check out the profiles of the people they have hired. Look to see what their employment history has been. You may discover some useful strategies for your own personal career goals, especially if you are starting out.

For example, you can look for trends in past work history within certain departments of a company. You might also discover a trend toward hiring employees who work outside of the traditional office environment and use technology to create the work environment instead.

Get to Know Hiring Managers

When you search for jobs, pay extra special attention to those jobs where a hiring manager is a 2nd or 3rd degree connection. Someone you know is acquainted with the person who posted the job. This is an opportunity you should not ignore.

If your connection is willing to recommend you, you may be able to set up an informational interview in person or over the phone.

If you don't have any direct connections, use LinkedIn to identify who the hiring manager is. To increase your chance of success, direct your application properly.

Another strategy you can use is to find a connection within the company who is willing to walk your application to the hiring manager's desk. HR doesn't have to know the person handing the resume over. Just the fact that the person works within the company can help your resume get attention.

Most companies don't spell out all the things they are really looking for in an applicant. Find a company connection within your network can help you acquire inside information about a listed position. You might also find out about non-posted opportunities.

Consider Startups

LinkedIn is a place where new companies are seeking exposure. Use search to locate startup opportunities. Try both the Company and other Filters, as the results will change. Since job security with large corporations is a thing of the past, consider startup opportunities, if your finances support it.

Remember, LinkedIn is a social site – the more you put into it, the more you will get out of it. Get in the habit of using LinkedIn to research opportunities and make connections with individuals who can help your job search.

When you have a job interview lined up, search for the interviewer on LinkedIn if you know their name. See who you know in common, and research the interviewer's background. Review the company page as well, and see if you have any connections with current employees.

Stay up to date with the latest happenings on LinkedIn too. Follow their official blog at: http://blog.linkedin.com/ Remember to always give! It will come back to you in some way.

DON'T MAKE THESE LINKEDIN MISTAKES

Don't Dismiss LinkedIn as Something Only for People Who Are Looking for a New Job.

The best time to build your LinkedIn profile, connect with people, and participate on LinkedIn is before you need it. If you find yourself suddenly unemployed and decide that now is the time to start using LinkedIn, you're going to be playing catch up. Instead, take time to "dig your well before you're thirsty", as author Harvey Mackay says.

Don't "Set it and Forget it."

Your LinkedIn profile is an evolving snapshot of you. You should be updating it regularly with new connections, status updates, and activity (within LinkedIn Groups particularly).

Check in on LinkedIn regularly – at least every other day if you are in active job search mode or at least once a week if you are a passive job seeker. Plan to add one new status update each time you log in.

Don't Forget to Explore the People Your Connections Know.

One of the most powerful functions of LinkedIn is the ability to connect you with people who are connections of the people you know. Follow LinkedIn's guidelines on connecting with these folks (using InMail or requesting connections through your mutual friend) so that your account is not flagged for spam.

Don't Be a Wallflower.

LinkedIn is most effective when you engage with it. Seek out opportunities to connect with thought leaders in your industry. Join 3-5 Groups and participate in conversations.

Don't Be Selfish.

You will get more out of LinkedIn if you focus on how you can help others, not how they can help you. The phrase "give to get" is very powerful and relevant on LinkedIn. You can earn the respect of your peers and people of influence if you "help enough other people get what they want," in the words of Zig Ziglar.

Don't Wait for Others to find You.

Use the LinkedIn People Search function to look for people you know and invite them to connect with you. You should aim to add 2-5 new connections each week if you are a passive job seeker and 6-10 connections a week if you are actively searching for a new job.

Don't Forget to Check Out "Daily Rundown".

Every morning in your Notifications section there is a collection of news stories that LinkedIn recommends to you. Check these out to stay abreast of important information in your industry and on current events. LinkedIn includes hashtags so you can share your thoughts.

Don't Restrict Your LinkedIn Networking to Online Only.

Use LinkedIn to connect with people, but then request in-person get-togethers, when it makes sense. Meet for coffee or lunch to catch up.

Don't try to Connect with People Indiscriminately.

One of the strengths of LinkedIn is the connections you make, but it's not a race to get 500+ connections. Have a reason for each person with whom you connect – either it's someone you already know or related to, or someone beneficial to connect with.

If you don't know someone, take time to get to know the person before sending a personalized connection request. (You can also see if you share any connections in common or by checking out their LinkedIn summary and work history, visiting their website or blog, and viewing which Groups s/he belongs to.)

Resources to Make Your Job Search on LinkedIn Easier

Interview Readiness

15-SecondPitch.com

This site will help you trim your elevator speech so you are ready for those calls.

Zoominfo.com

This is a great site for locating companies and doing your background research.

Join.me

This website makes it easy to set up client conferences and screen sharing.

Social Media Management

Hootsuite.com

There is a fee to use this service, but if you want to manage social media profiles on several sites, this is a very efficient way to do it.

Tweetdeck.com

This is a free web application that can be installed on your computer. There are versions for iPhone, Android, and Chrome. It will allow you to manage social media connections on LinkedIn, Twitter, Facebook, and Google+

Engaging Profile

Tinyurl.com | Bitly.com

These are link-shortening services.

Optimization Tools

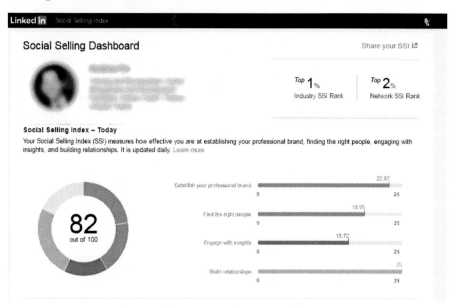

LinkedIn SSI

LinkedIn Social Selling Index. This is a part of LinkedIn that you won't find ON LinkedIn. It's associated with LinkedIn's

Sales Navigator product. You might be asking: "What does Sales Navigator have to do with my job search? Wel,l if your job while you're in job search is sales and marketing and you're the product then might a sales tool associated with LinkedIn and your LinkedIn profile be helpful? Yes, especially when your **SSI Score** is determined by: **Establishing your professional brand, Finding the right people, Engaging with insights** and **Building relationships.** We've been discussing these topics throughout this whole book. You get a score out of 100 which is measured against these four areas and it changes daily. It's a great bench mark to see who effectively you're utilizing LinkedIn in these four areas.

jobscan.co

This is a service offering both free and paid options to help optimize both your resume and LinkedIn profile compared to the types of positions you are interested in by using the job descriptions for those positions and comparing them against your resume or LinkedIn profile.

wordle.net

The site describes itself as a "toy". What it does is generate word clouds based on word repetition. What you can also do though is copy and paste a job description into it, generate the word cloud and that will show you visually what words are used the most in the Job Description. This will give a good idea of what words the companies are using a lot to talk about what they are looking for in a candidate. You can use this for both resumes and your LinkedIn profile.

photofeeler.com

Review research into what makes a great profile photo and even upload your own photos to get a sense of how influential, competent, or likable you appear in it.

ABOUT THE AUTHORS

Fred Coon

Founder, Chairman, and CEO
fcoon@stewartcoopercoon.com

 Fred Coon is founder, CEO and President of Stewart, Cooper & Coon. He started SC&C as an Executive Search firm and grew the company into five divisions. In that process he has advised thousands of executives on their job search campaigns. Fred is quoted in Forbes, U.S. News & World Report, Money Magazine, Inc. Magazine, Success Magazine, The Wall Street Journal, and other major national publications, and appears on affiliate stations of ABC, NBC, and CBS as an expert on the job and employment market. His SC&C Career Advice Blog has over 5,000 monthly subscribers worldwide.

Fred was on the senior team of two different companies, in two different industries, achieving multiple listings in Inc. Magazine's top 500 fastest growing companies in America. One of those companies, Certified Collateral Corporation, was in the top 100 fastest growing companies in the United States. CCC was number 31 on the 1986 Inc. Magazine 100 List and number 54 on the 1987 Inc. Magazine 100 List, as well as first in profitability among all of the listed companies in both years.

He is a Licensed Employment Agent, a Nationally Certified Job and Career Transition Coach, a Behavioral Consultant and a Certified Disc Administrator. Mr. Coon is a member of the Arizona Technology Council – Policy Advisory Committee, the Workforce Business Intelligence Board, and The Forbes Coaching Council.

He is a founding member of The Arizona Corporate Council on Veteran Careers. This is a collaboration of companies focused on maximizing career opportunities for all service members, veterans and their family members statewide. The corporate council works in partnership with the Arizona Department of Veterans' Services, the Arizona Coalition for Military Families and other key stakeholders in support of the Arizona Roadmap to Veteran Employment.

He is author of two best-selling career books, Ready Aim Hired, and Leveraging LinkedIn For Job Search Success. At this writing his first edition of Leveraging LinkedIn has over 40,000 copies in the marketplace. Mr. Coon is a contributing author to the book, Business Model You, by Tim Clark, which is currently printed in seven languages. His latest book, Hire The EQ, Not The IQ, was released in 2018. This book focuses on hiring the right "fit" for any given job using behavioral interviewing tactics that he and his co-author, Ron Venckus, spent 10 years researching and developing behavioral questions that will help managers hire the right fit for any given job.

Concurrently, he is authoring a military transition book specifically directed at anyone leaving the Armed Forces who would like to better understand how to make a personally meaningful and financially rewarding transition. He lectures and conducts hand-on workshops throughout United States for universities, educational, professional, business and management conferences and on military installations, nationwide.

On a personal note, he is also a well-known 5-string Appalachian claw-hammer style banjo player with concert performances in Ireland, Scotland, England, Australia, and throughout the United States, with media appearances on local, regional, and international radio and television programs, both in the U.S. and overseas, for over five decades.

Andrew R. Ko

Andrew is an executive recruiter and executive career coach. He

is a credentialed Global Career Development Facilitator. He also has a certification in Training Gamification as well as holds certifications from Dale Carnegie Training and a certificate in Emotional Intelligence. He has experience leading career development, training and development, outplacement, and leadership development. Andrew pulls back the curtain on job search with his clients and helps them land their next job faster. Andrew's professional background includes over 10 years with a Fortune 500 company and he leverages this corporate experience to better serve his clients.

Andrew also has a background working with the military veteran community and has been awarded for his work with a well-known and respected non-profit focused on working with veterans to help them find employment. He is credited for creating and developing a career development training program to better serve their veteran clients.

He is a member of the Association of Talent Development and a member of the National Association of Workforce Development Professionals where he has been a primary presenter for several of their national conventions on subjects such as Career Development and LinkedIn.

Andrew is also a published artist. When not working in recruiting and career development he enjoys art and has sold his artwork in several solo exhibits around Los Angeles. He also has several certifications in search and rescue and has spent four years on a volunteer search and rescue team and enjoys hiking.

Kelly Stewart

Kelly Stewart has been in the 'people' field for more than 20 years. Her background combines personal branding and corporate hu-

man resources expertise plus best-in-class certifications. Her clients benefit by maximizing their strengths, understanding their unique value, and attracting the opportunities they deserve throughout their careers.

Kelly began to use LinkedIn in its infancy in 2007. At that time, the tool had only 10M users. Kelly understood the value of LinkedIn as the new 'professional' Rolodex. She created classes and began teaching LinkedIn to outplacement audiences and other groups in 2008 and has since been a 'power user' of this networking imperative. Currently, there are over 570M (Q3, 2018) users worldwide, and it is the #1 resource for online professional networking. Kelly has worked with thousands of professionals to authentically establish their online presence and teach them to utilize LinkedIn as a vital career development tool.

Kelly's career encompasses more than 14 years of success in Human Resources for Fortune 500 firms. She possesses core competencies in coaching, recruiting, talent management, leadership development, employer branding, and as an HR Business Partner. In 2008, Kelly leveraged this rich foundational experience by launched her own firm. She is known for applying personal branding techniques in coaching career successes and developing impressive branded career-marketing materials.

She holds an MA, Human Resource Management, BA, Communications and English. Her certifications include: Global Professional in Human Resources (GPHR), Associate Certified Coach, (ACC), Leadership and Talent Management Coach (CLTMC), Career Coach (CCMC), Certified Personal Brand Strategist (CPBS), Online Identity Strategist (COIS), and as a professional résumé writer (CPRW).

Originally from New Jersey, Kelly currently resides in Raleigh, North Carolina. She enjoys cooking, Pilates, TRX, and spending time with her husband, two sons, and Labrador retriever (preferably at the beach).

SOURCES

Block, Jay. *A Picture's Worth a Thousand Words? FALSE!* "Spotlight." Professional Association of Resume Writers & Career Coaches, March 2015, 7–9.

Hempel, Jessi. Last modified March 24, 2010. Money.cnn.com/2010/03/24/technology/ linkedin_social_networking.fortune/.

LinkedIn. (2014, August). LinkedIn Help Center. Retrieved from https://help.linkedin.com/app/answers/detail/ a_id/5023/kw/outlook+contacts+import/related.

LinkedIn Talent Solutions. *Build Your Personal Brand on LinkedIn.* Last modified February 2015. https://business.linkedin.com/talentsolutions/c/14/ 12/build-your-personal-brand-on-linkedin-g.

Wynkoop, Kooper. *The Importance of LinkedIn During a Job Search | Jobfully Blog.* Jobfully Blog. Free Resources for Job Seekers to Help Them Find a Job Faster and Easier. Accessed March 9, 2015. http://blog.jobfully.com/2012/05/linkedin-and-job-search/.

INDEX

A

B

C

D

N

Notifications 80

P

People Search 67, 74, 154
Photos
change 31
photo 16, 19, 25, 26, 31, 33, 34, 38, 65, 72, 79, 149, 159
photograph 18, 33, 34
professional photograph 18
profile picture 33
upload 16, 25, 26, 31, 32, 58, 90, 146, 159
Power Tip 11, 122
Privacy 69
changing settings 72
privacy settings 4, 69, 72, 74, 79, 149
Profile
All-Star profile 66
certifications 41, 61, 77, 163, 164, 165
edit / enhance 23
editing / branding 38
education 12, 19, 20, 24, 52, 61, 62, 65, 77, 143, 162
experience section 58
headline 34
keywords 4, 10, 20, 22, 34, 39, 40, 41, 42, 43, 50, 53, 60, 66, 67,
    68, 71, 93, 104, 122, 123, 124, 127, 128, 134, 136, 137, 140,
    150
personal website 66
public profile 69, 72, 74
references 48, 51, 52, 103, 120
share profile 77
Skills 3, 26, 50, 77, 105
strengths 19, 20, 24, 66
summary 3, 28, 39, 52, 55, 143, 148
work samples 4, 58
years of experience 31

R

Recommendations
removing recommendations 5, 111
requests 5, 120
testimonial 3, 47, 54
writing recommendations 114